Alto's

Creative Mat Designs

Design Collection 2

Publisher: Alto's EZ Mat, Inc.
          703 N. Wenas St.
          Ellensburg, WA 98926–2861

Toll Free: 1–800–225–2497
Phone: 1–509–962–9212
Fax: 1–509–962–3127
email: altosmat@eburg.com
internet: www.altosezmat.com

© Alto's EZ Mat, Inc. 1998
ISBN 0–9658215–1–X
Printed in the U.S.A.

Reprints of the second twelve *CUT–by–CUT* designs from #0401 to #0506.

Introduction

Welcome to Creative Mat Designs, Design Collection II. In this volume you will find a review of the basic mat cutting techniques and step–by–step instructions on cutting eleven unusual and decorative mats.

With clear and easy to follow explanations we will lead you through cutting each mat design in a specific size. Then you can modify the dimensions to fit your particular pieces of artwork. Even better, we hope that you will expand upon these ideas in this book to create *your own* mat designs! Let us know what you come up with!

DETAILS OF A WELL CUT MAT

CORNERS

Cleanly cut corners are essential, with no curves, tears or obvious overcuts.

BORDERS

Many mats are cut with all borders of equal width. For a "weighted" mat effect, cut the bottom border wider than the top and sides.

DIMENSIONS

Proportioned for good balance. Cut to fit the artwork and frame.

EDGES

Inner edges should be clean and smooth, with a straight 45° bevel along the entire length of the cut.

SURFACES

Surfaces are clean, with no pencil or other marks. The mat color compliments the artwork.

MULTIPLE MATS

For mats with multiple layers, all cut edges must be perfectly parallel. Border and liner widths compliment the artwork and frame.

TOOLS AND MATERIALS NEEDED TO CUT ALL ELEVEN MATS

– Alto's 4501 or 4505 Mat Cutting System
– Alto's Oval Template Set
– Alto's Model 360 Circle Cutter
– Various colors of matboard
– Scrap pieces of matboard as cutting surfaces*
– Lots of sharp blades
– Sharp pencil
– Non–abrasive eraser
– Double–stick tape
– Acid–free white glue
– 45°–45°–90° triangle
– Ruler

For the Border Inlay Mat you will need
– A piece of decorative paper for the inlaid accents (at least 8-1/2" x 11")
– Sharp hobby knife
– Marker or pencil of similar color to the matboard.

*When using the Model 360 try using a piece of 3/4" plywood <u>under</u> your cutting surface.
3/4" plywood is flat and holds the centering tack secure.

It is important to be familiar with Alto's Mat Cutting Tools to master the designs of the book.

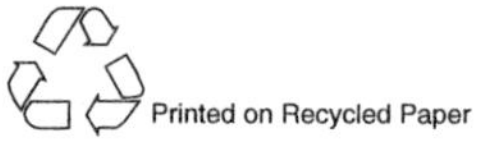
Printed on Recycled Paper

Table of Contents

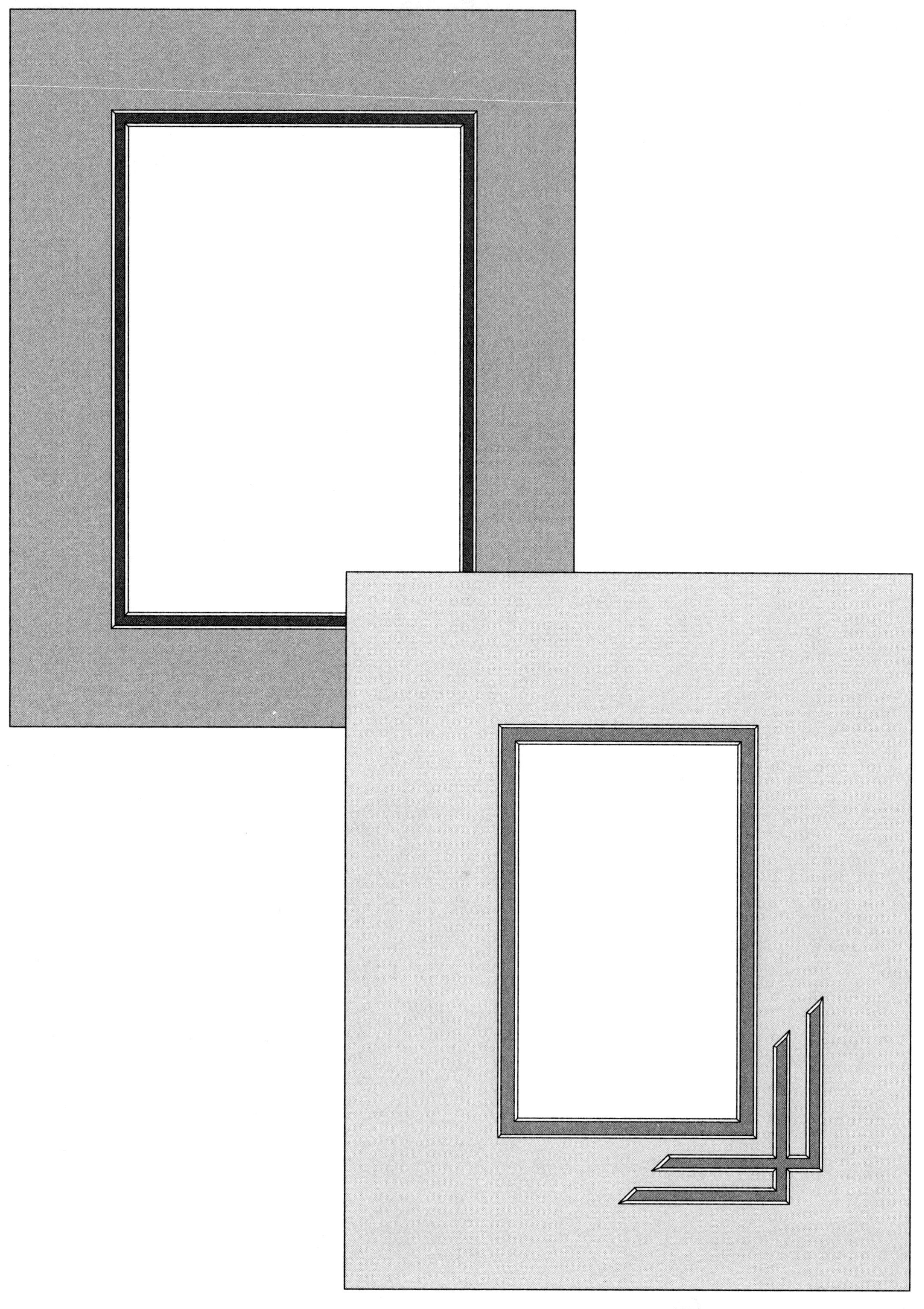

Review of the Basics

KEY POINTS FOR SUCCESSFUL MATTING: *Here are some of the basic key points to focus on when cutting any mat. Checking these for every mat you cut will raise your level of mat cutting.*

Sharp blades are essential. There are other blades made to the basic size of Alto's Model 45 blade, but Alto's blades are custom made just for mat cutting with a double honed edge to keep the blade cutting straight. Blades will dull at different rates depending on the matboard used. Matboards vary in thickness, core and surface. Black core is harder on blades than rag core. Also, complex mat designs with many cuts may require many blade changes, especially if the mat surface is fabric or the mat is black core. Remember to flip the blade to use both points. Generally, a new, sharp blade should last for approximately four to five average sized mats <u>per point</u>, when using rag matboard.

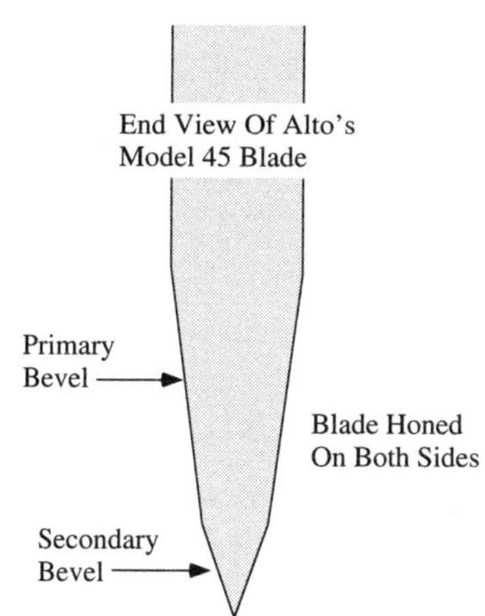

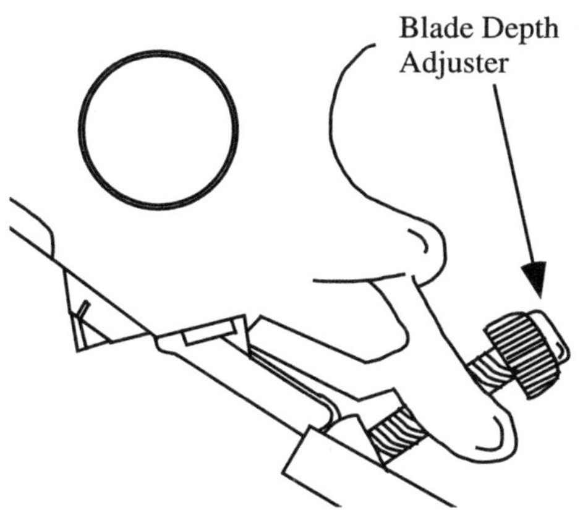

Correct blade depth. The blade should be set so that it cuts through the mat and slightly into the cutting surface underneath. When properly adjusted, your cut should be smooth and clean, not requiring excessive pressure. To adjust the blade depth of the Model 45, raise or lower the blade depth adjustment screw (see illustration).

> **CUTTING WITH A SHARP BLADE SET AT THE PROPER DEPTH DOES NOT REQUIRE EXCESSIVE FORCE.**

Even pressure as you cut. In order to have the blade cut all the way through the matboard, pivot the cutter head down so the end of the blade adjustment screw touches the cutter base and you are unable to pivot any further (see above illustration). Now the blade should be cutting through the matboard. *It is important not to allow the blade to lift during the cut.* As you cut, keep even pressure down and in, with the base of the Model 45 tight against the straightedge. If you are applying even pressure and the blade is not cutting through the matboard, then adjust the blade depth and check your start–stop positions.

Fresh cutting surface. CHANGE YOUR CUTTING SURFACE FREQUENTLY. The cutting surface is the matboard fastened to the base unit of your Alto's Mat Cutting System. After you have cut several mats you will need to change or relocate your cutting surface. Other names for this cutting surface are "underlayment" or "slip sheet". Scrap matboard cut to the appropriate size makes an excellent replacement.

Little grooves in this cutting surface left by previous cuts can pull the blade off course. These grooves also allow the surface paper of the mat being cut to be pushed out by the blade instead of cutting it cleanly. This causes a ragged or fuzzy edge on the mat window. Prevent this by moving the cutting surface so the blade will cut into a fresh area on the cutting surface. Because cuts are repeated in the same place, self–healing cutting surfaces do not work.

Cutting a Basic Single Mat

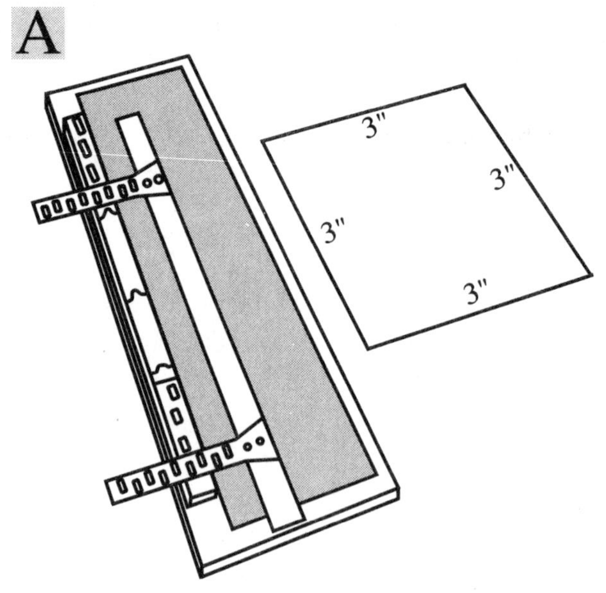

*N*o matter how experienced you are, a review and perfecting of the basics will improve any advanced design you are cutting.

Tools and materials needed
– Alto's 4501 or 4505 Mat Cutting System
– One piece of 11" x 14" matboard
– Sharp blade
– Sharp pencil

1 **Write border widths on the back of your matboard.** To prevent cutting mistakes, you may want to write border settings on the mat (see Diagram A) as a reminder to reset the dimensioning system later. For this exercise, use 3" for all four sides **(Diagram A)**.

2 **Set the Cutting Guide.** Set the dimensioning system at the desired border width (3" for this exercise). For best results and better visibility, work standing at a waist–high table. Press down on the end of the arm to raise the cutting guide. Slide the matboard (back side up) under the cutting guide until it butts firmly against the stops **(Diagram B)**.

3 **Draw start/stop reference lines.** Make sure the matboard is back side up. Pencil a line along the cutting guide the length of your matboard. Rotate your matboard to the next side, reinsert it under the cutting guide and pencil another line **(Diagram C)**.
These four lines are your start and stop reference lines. Leave matboard in place against the stops.
NOTE: If the desired border is less than 1-1/2" wide, (see 4501 and 4505 Mat Cutting System Instructions, "Cutting Narrow Borders" p. 13.)

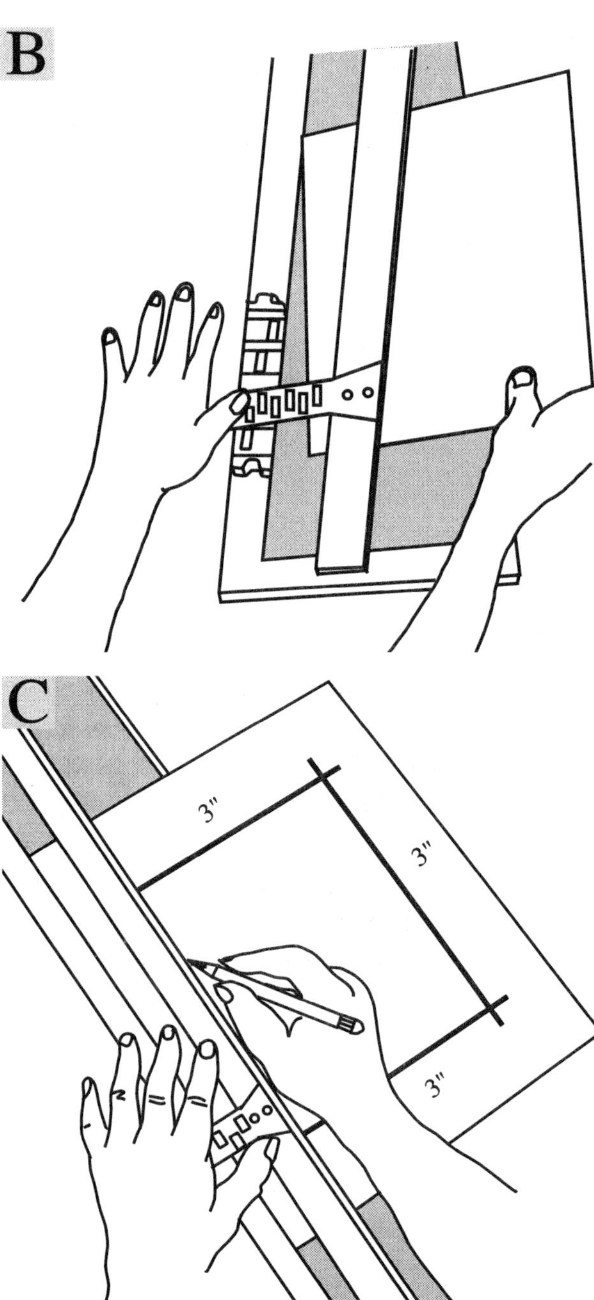

Review of the Basics

4 **Place Model 45 against the cutting guide.**
Position it so that the tip of the blade touches the
start reference line (the *horizontal* line closest to you)
when handle is pivoted downward (**Diagram D**).
DO NOT CUT YET.

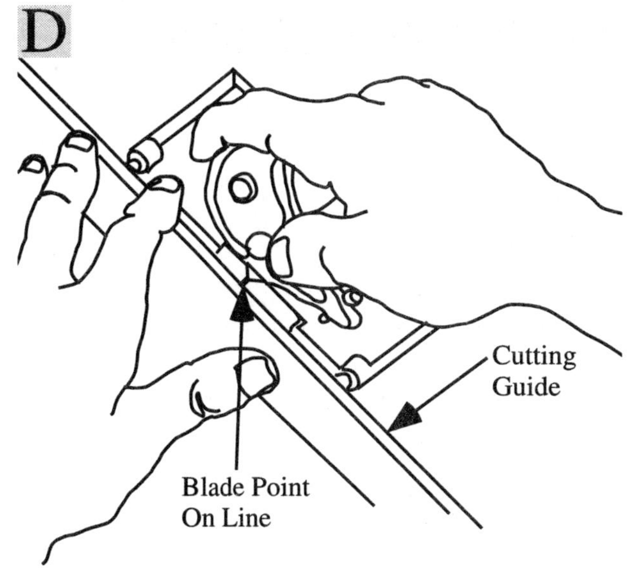

5 **Pivot the blade completely down and in at the
start line.** To cut, push the cutter forward, keeping
even downward pressure on the blade (**Diagram E**).
Make sure the cutter rides flush against the
straightedge. Press down on the straightedge with your
other hand to secure the matboard while you are
cutting. *The cut should feel smooth, without excessive
force.* Use just enough downward pressure to hold the
blade down securely.

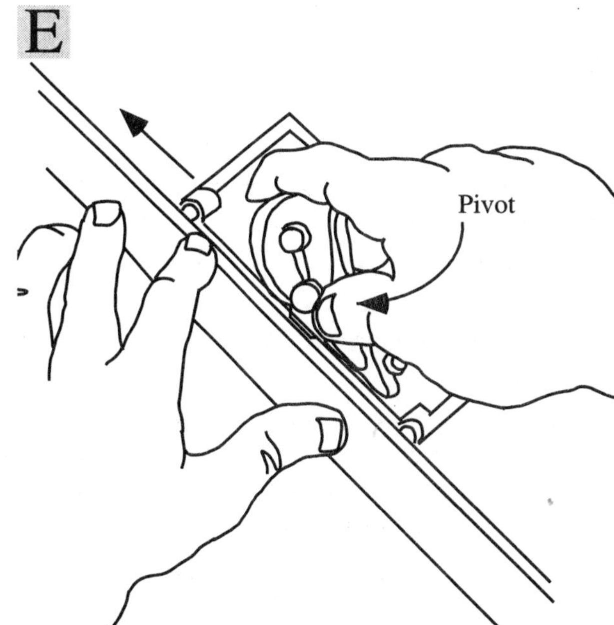

6 **Stop cutting when the <u>silver</u> <u>mark</u> on the blade
holder is over the stop reference line, the
horizontal pencil line farthest from you
(Diagram F).** The silver mark indicates the cutting
edge of the blade. Rotate your matboard to the next
side and adjust the system if your border widths vary.
Repeat until all four sides are cut. After you have
made your fourth cut, the window should fall freely
from your mat.

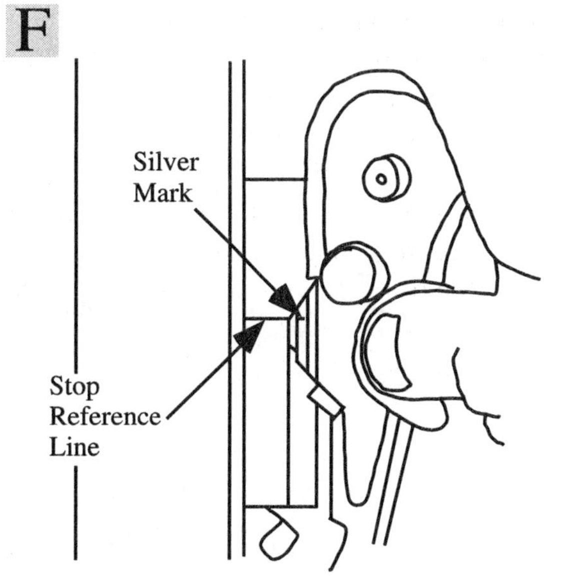

Ilf the window doesn't fall out, be careful not to
tear it out.** Reinsert the mat (back side up) under
the cutting guide and recut the uncut edges or corners.
Be sure the cutter is pivoted all the way down during
the entire cut. If necessary, set your blade slightly
deeper. If the window scrap isn't consistently falling
free because the corners are not cutting through, start
your cut slightly before the start line and stop your cut
slightly past the stop line. Remember you are cutting a
45° bevel cut. *Cuts must intersect to create perfect
corners.*

**If you didn't cut through the corners completely, do
not tear the window out.** Turn the matboard over and
carefully cut through the remaining material with a
sharp blade **(Diagram G)**.

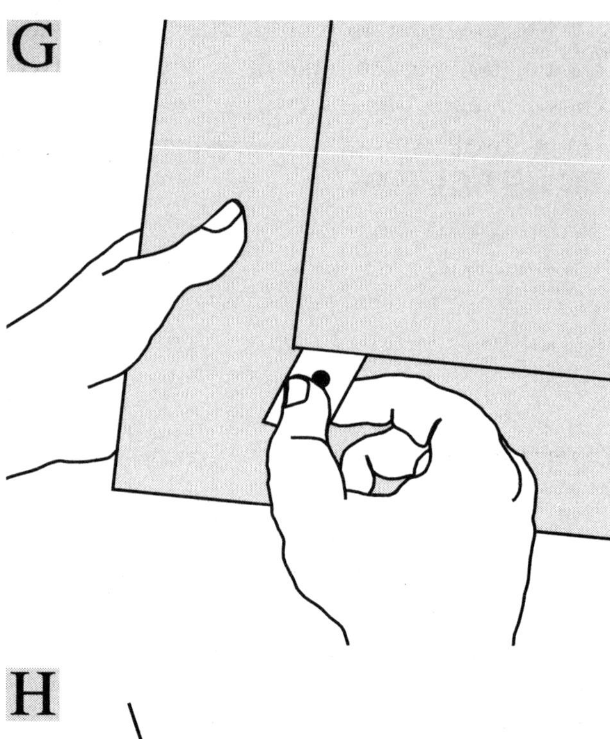

Fine Start/Stop Adjustments. The thickness of your
matboard will determine where you start and stop your
cuts. For very thick matboard you will need to start
your cut ahead of the start reference line and stop your
cut further beyond the stop reference line.

**Notice that your cuts are not directly along the start
and stop reference lines (Diagram H).** Don't worry,
these lines only act as reference marks for starting and
stopping your cuts. The actual window is cut to fit
your artwork as you determined in Step 1. The Alto's
system is engineered to cross the cuts on the back of
the matboard to give you a perfect corner on the front.

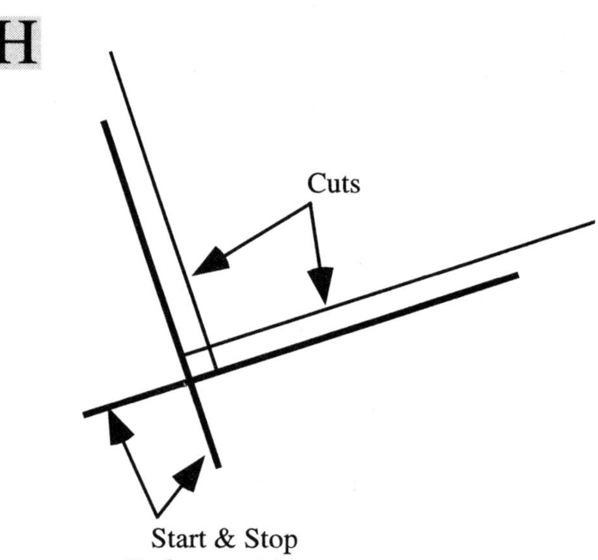

Cutting left–handed. Turn the whole system around
180 degrees, so that the arms point to the right. Figure
border widths and draw start and stop reference lines as
shown for cutting a single mat. To cut left–handed,
you will **pull the cutter toward you rather than push
it away from you.** Place Model 45 against the
straightedge as shown. The palm of your left hand
rests on the front of the cutter handle (the end with the
Model 45 emblem) and your fingers wrap around the
handle. Start your cut at the far horizontal line and
stop your cut at the horizontal line closest to you. Use
even pressure down and into the blade and keep the
cutter flush with the straightedge **(Diagram I)**.
Practice on a few pieces of scrap matboard to perfect
the technique.

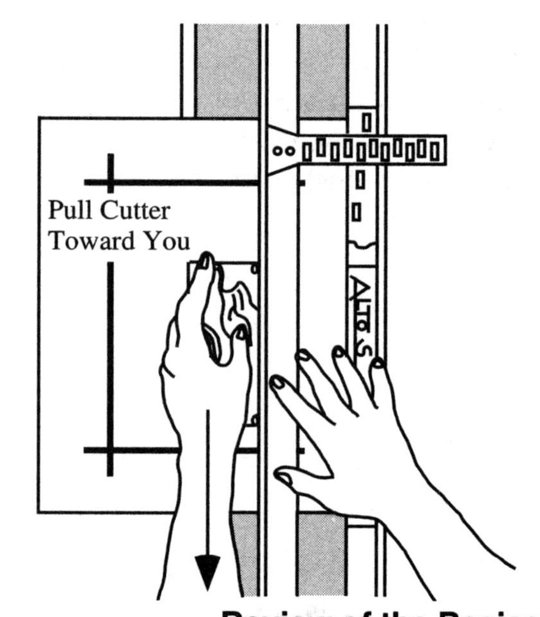

Review of the Basics

Checking corners. Take a good look at the corners
on the first few mats you cut. With your Alto's
System, your mats should have straight 45° beveled
edges, square corners and minimal or no overcuts.

Look at the corners cut on the front of the mat and
flip the mat over to the back side and look at the
reference lines drawn. It is important to understand the
relationship between the cuts on the front of the mat
and the pencil lines drawn on the back of the mat.
This is where the fine cutting adjustments are made.

Overcuts. Slight overcuts help ensure perfectly square
corners and are acceptable by most professional picture
framing standards (**Diagram J**). Excessive overcuts
are undesirable (**Diagram K**). For the correct amount
of overcut, you may need to adjust where you start and
stop your cuts, depending on the thickness of your
matboard. Thicker matboard requires that you start a
little more before the start reference line and stop a
little past the stop reference line.

To conceal overcuts. A burnishing bone or a smooth
rounded piece of plastic can be used to press on the
overcuts and the overcuts will practically disappear.
Be sure to rub lightly. Excessive pressure will leave
the surface noticeably shiny. **Or you may gently
press on the overcut with a corner of the same
matboard used for the mat.** Push the raised overcut
back to the level of the mat. In most cases, the overcut
disappears to all but close scrutiny.

To conceal torn edges. If your cut was made with a
blade that was not as sharp as it should have been, you
might get some tearing of the top color. **If the tearing
is not excessive, try gently rubbing on the rough
edge with the flat surface of your window fall out,
color side against color side (Diagram L).**

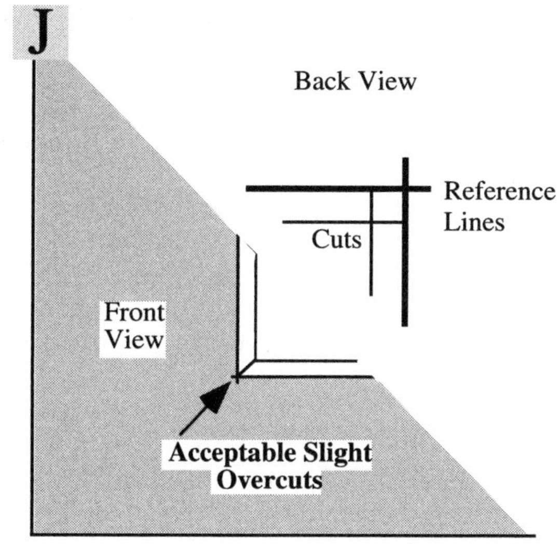

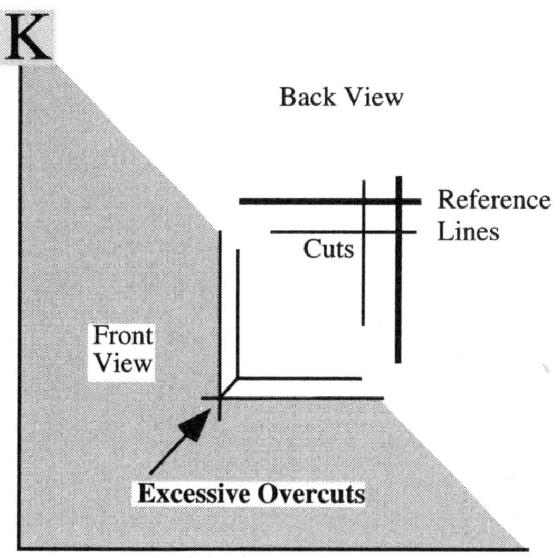

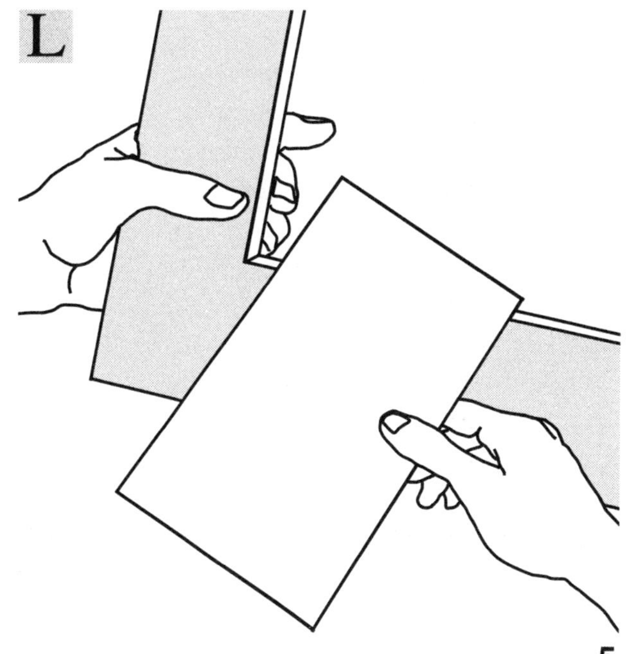

Cathedral

This double mat is done in four stages. First, draw all lines on the back of the mat. Second, cut the arc. Third, cut the straight cuts. Fourth and last, repeat the whole process with a 1/2" difference in the arc measurements and a 1/4" difference in measurements for the liner.

Tools and materials needed
- Alto's 4501 or 4505 Mat Cutting System
- Alto's Model 360 Circle Cutter
- Two pieces of 11" x 14" matboard in complementary colors. Make sure that the two pieces are <u>exactly</u> the same size.
- Cutting surface*
- Sharp blades
- Sharp pencil
- Double–stick tape

*When using the Model 360 try using a piece of 3/4" plywood <u>under</u> your cutting surface. 3/4" plywood is flat and holds the centering tack secure.

Top Mat

1 Set the dimensioning system at 5-5/8", and the long side of mat back side up against the stops, draw an approximately 3" long line about 3" from the top edge of the mat as shown (Diagram A). Rotate mat 180° and draw another line in the same place.

NOTE: If this line matches the first one you drew, then 5-5/8" is indeed the center of the mat. If there is a space between the lines, then the center is halfway between them.

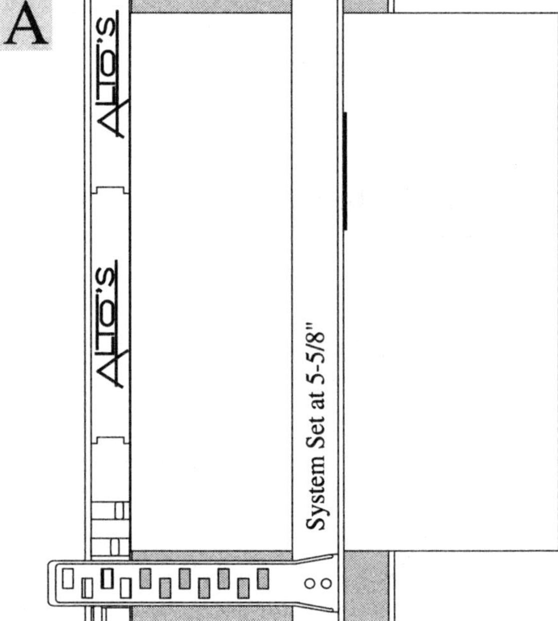

Design: Cathedral

2 **Rotate mat 90° and set the system at 5".** Draw a short line crossing the centerline(s) you just drew **(Diagram B)**.

3 **Leave mat in same position. Set the system at 4". Draw two approximately 2" lines starting an inch from each edge as shown (Diagram B).**

4 **Set the system at 2".** Rotate the matboard as needed to draw three reference lines for the window opening. Two of these 2" lines will stop at the two lines from Step 3 as shown **(Diagram B)**.

5 **Place the bottom mat under the top mat with the backs of both facing up. Line them up exactly.** Place them flat on the cutting surface and push the centering tack through both mats, at exactly the center of the crossed lines you drew in Step 2 **(Diagram C)**. **NOTE:** If the two lines you drew in Step 1 were different, push tack through the cross line at a point halfway between them.

6 **Remove the tack and set the bottom mat aside. Turn over the top mat so the color side is face up.** Place the centering tack in the Model 360 hole marked 6". Then place tack (while in cutter) into the hole, through the <u>front of the matboard</u>.

7 **Cut an arc in the top of the mat as shown, greater than 180° (Diagram D).** Turn mat over.

Make sure to cut your arc greater than 180°, but don't cut a full circle.

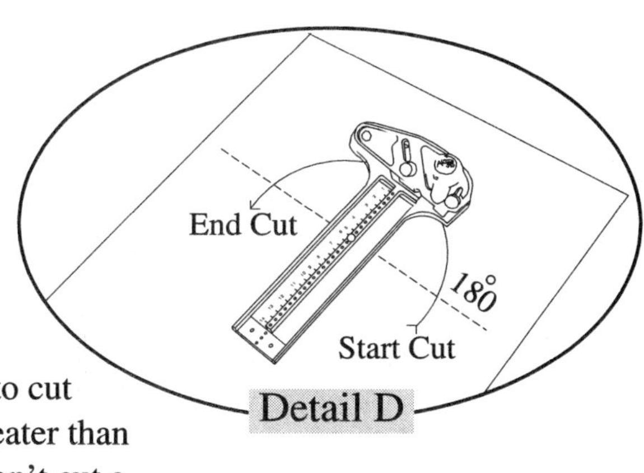

B

C

D

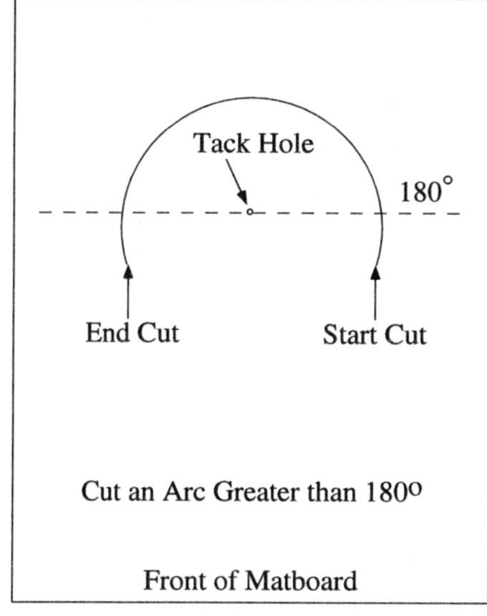

8 **Set the system at 4" and cut the two lines drawn at this setting.** For the first, start at the window opening reference line and cut past the arc, and for the second, start before the arc and cut to the window opening reference line (**Diagram E**).

9 **Set the system at 2" and cut the remaining three sides of the window opening.** NOTE: If the window piece does not fall out, use an inserted razor blade to finish the straight cuts, (see page 4, Diagram G). If the arc is not cut completely through, you will have to reinsert the tack and recut. Set the top mat aside.

BOTTOM MAT

10 **Set the system at 4-1/4".** Draw two short lines as you did on the top mat, from the window opening lines toward the tack hole as shown (**Diagram F**).

11 **Set the system at 2-1/4".** Rotate the matboard as needed to draw the three window opening reference lines, omitting the side of the mat with the tack hole and 4-1/4" lines (**Diagram F**).

12 **Turn the mat over, color side up.** Place the centering tack in the Model 360 hole marked 5-1/2". Then place tack (while in cutter) into the hole, through the <u>front of the matboard</u>.

13 **Cut an arc greater than 180° at the top of the mat** (and opposite the window opening reference lines drawn on the back, refer to Diagram D). Turn mat over.

14 **Set the system back at 4-1/4".** Cut the two lines drawn at this setting just as you did for the first mat in Step 8 (refer to Diagram E).

15 **Set the system at 2-1/4" and cut the remaining three sides of the window opening.** Again, if window piece does not fall out, use razor blade or Model 360 to complete cuts.

16 **Place double–stick tape on the back side of the top mat.** Permanently adhere it to the front side of the bottom mat, being very careful to align the mats accurately (**Diagram G**).

E

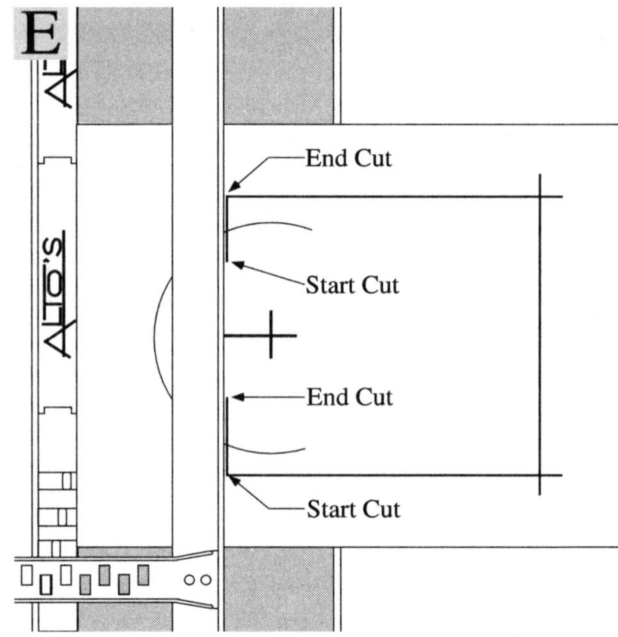

F

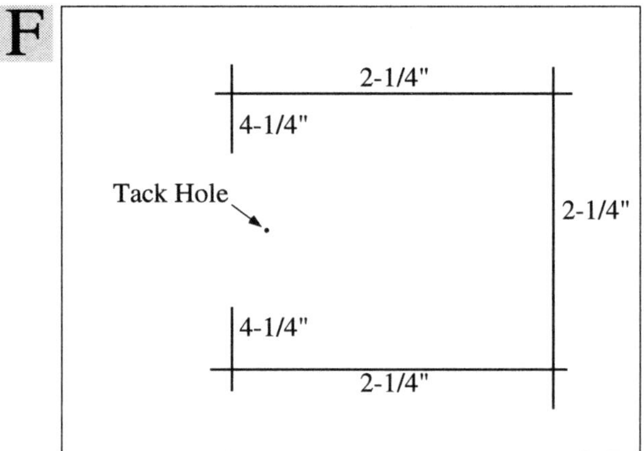

G

Design: Cathedral

Now that you've conquered combining straight cuts with arcs, try some of these variations, or create your own!

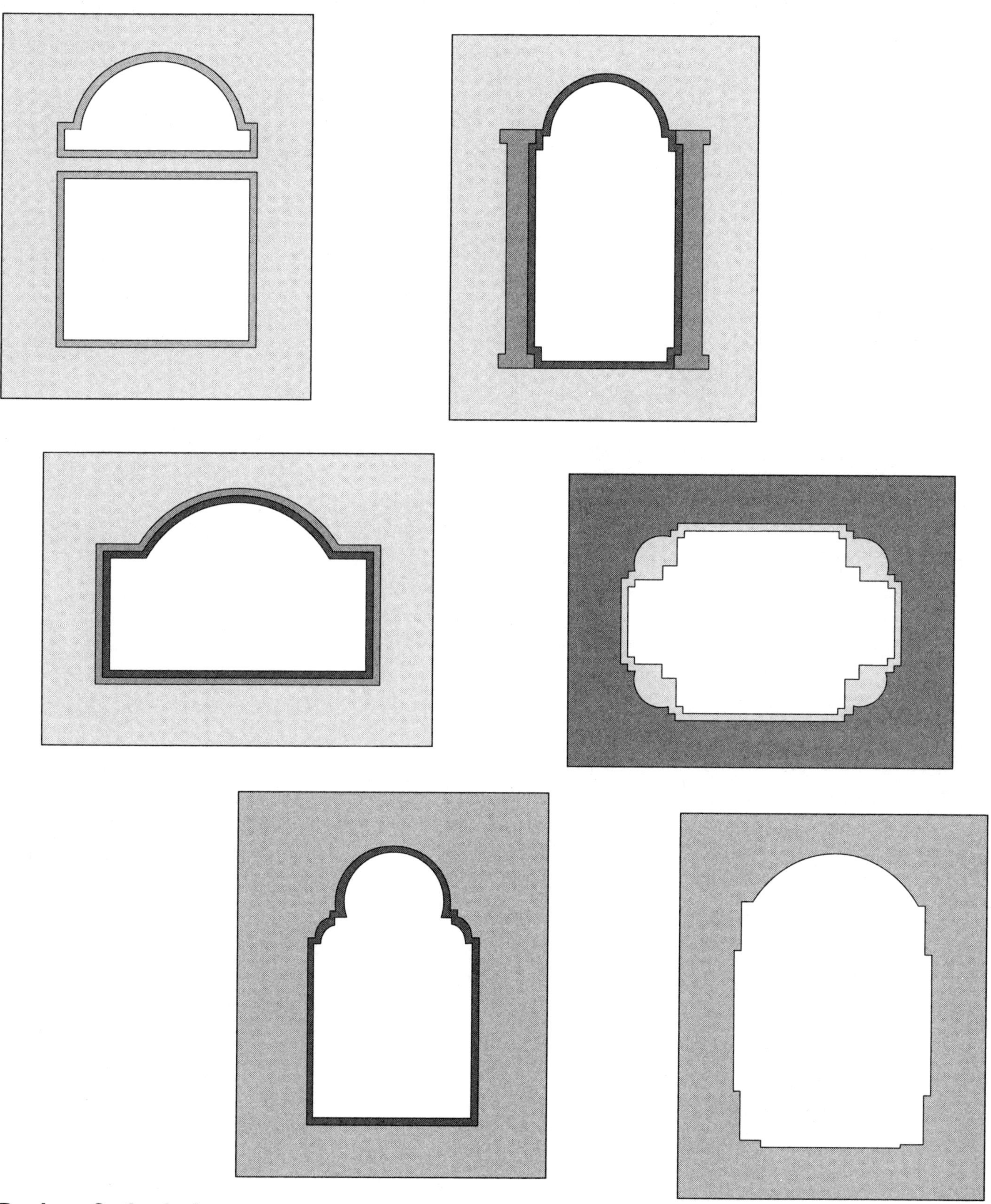

Design: Cathedral

Triple Ovals

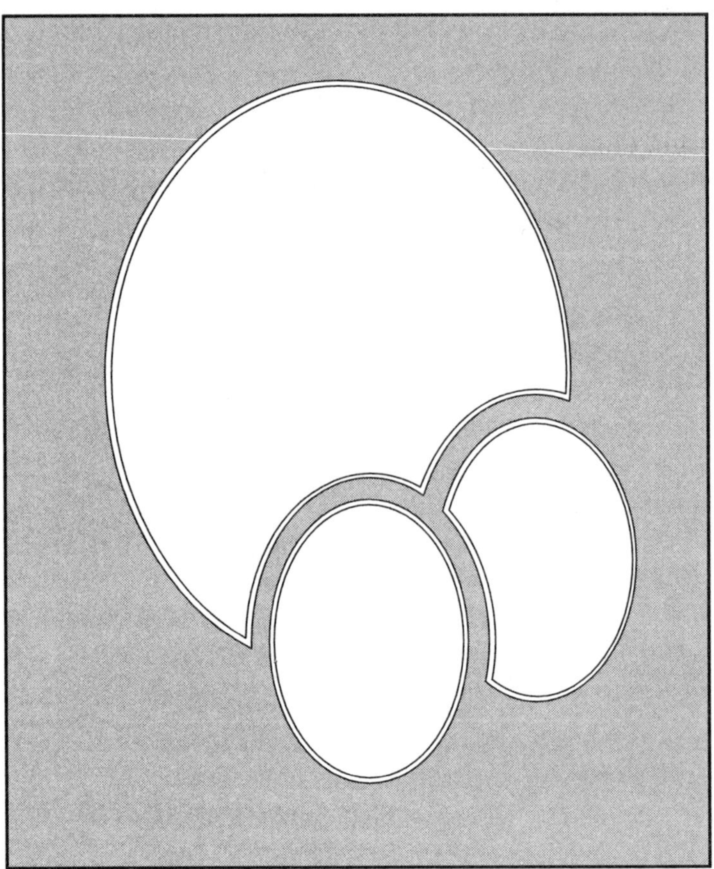

We'll make this mat in two stages: first, *we'll draw a series of lines to determine what we wish to cut and what we need to remain uncut. Second, we'll cut the mat.* Sounds simple? Well it <u>is</u>, and here are specific step–by–step instructions. Learn this pattern on a practice matboard first.

Tools and materials needed
  – Alto's Oval Template Set
  – One 16" x 20" piece of matboard
  – Scrap pieces of matboard as a cutting surface
  – Sharp blade
  – Sharp pencil
  – Non–abrasive eraser

A standard piece of 32" x 40" matboard cut into four equal pieces will yield four pieces of the proper size for cutting this mat.

NOTE: When cutting this mat, you will be using the oval templates without some of the tacks designed to hold them securely. Therefore, when cutting, hold the templates securely with one hand while cutting with the other.

DRAWING THE MAT

1 **Remove the bottom tack from the #4 oval template.** Place template on the *colored* side of the matboard approximately 2" from the top and from the left edges of the matboard as shown **(Diagram A)**. Pound the remaining three tacks to secure template to mat and cutting surface. With a sharp pencil, lightly draw around the entire oval template **(Diagram A)**. Remove the template.

A 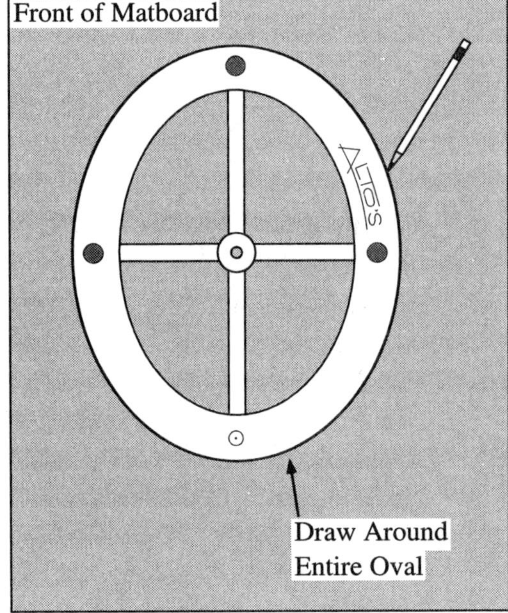

Design: Triple Ovals

2 **Remove both the bottom and left tacks from the #2 oval template.** *Place the template overlapping the line you drew around the large oval*, so that the right edge of the #2 template is approximately 2" from the right edge of the matboard as shown, and the bottom of the template is no more than 1" lower than the bottom of the big oval (**Diagram B**). This is Position A for the small right oval. Pound in the two remaining tacks.

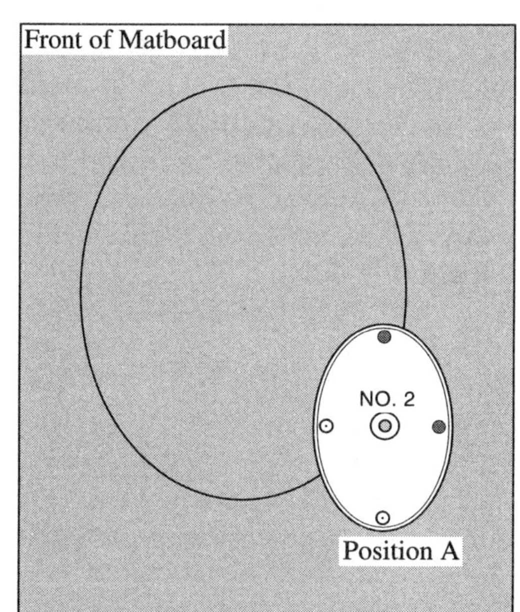

3 **With a pencil, lightly draw around the entire oval (Diagram C).**

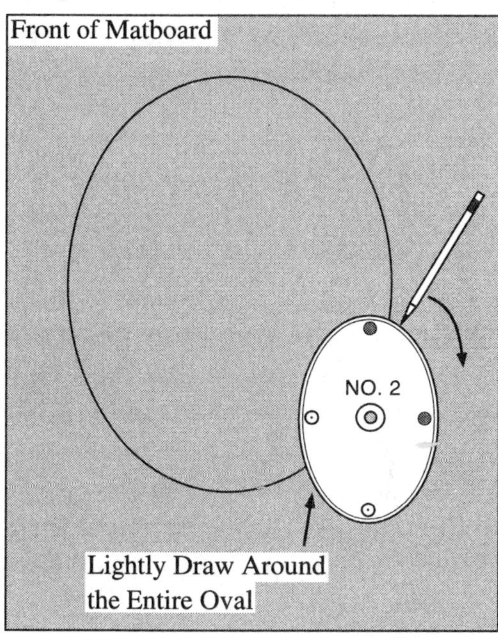

4 **Using the liner tool, place pencil point in the second hole from the bottom in the first row of holes on the right (See detail).** *Place liner tool against template and lightly draw around the portion of the small oval that is within the big oval, going past the big oval on the right by an inch* (**Diagram D**). Remove template.

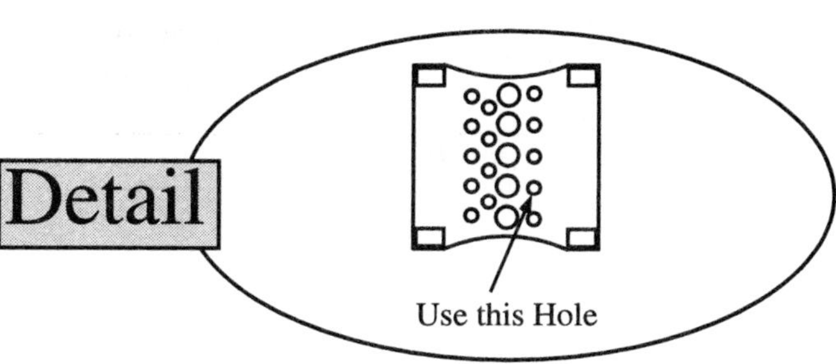

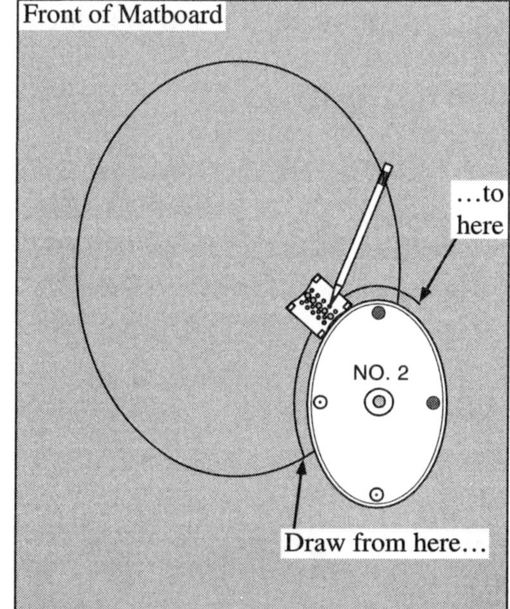

5 Place the #2 template below Position A, so that it overlaps the big oval by 2" to 3", but overlaps the small oval by only 1/2" (this is to prevent a greater overlap that will compromise the photo or artwork in the right small oval). This will be Position B for the left small oval. Pound in the two tacks **(Diagram E)**.

6 Using the same hole in the liner tool, draw all but the bottom segment of the oval as shown **(Diagram F)**.

7 Remove the oval template and flip the matboard *over to the back* so that the small ovals are still toward the bottom of the mat. Remove the right tack of the #2 oval and replace it in the left side of the template. **Place the #2 template so that the tacks are in the holes you made in Step 2 for Position A.** Pound the tacks in. Draw around the entire oval **(No Diagram)**.

8 Using the same liner tool hole as in Step 4, draw around the upper right quadrant of the template as shown **(Diagram G)**.

E

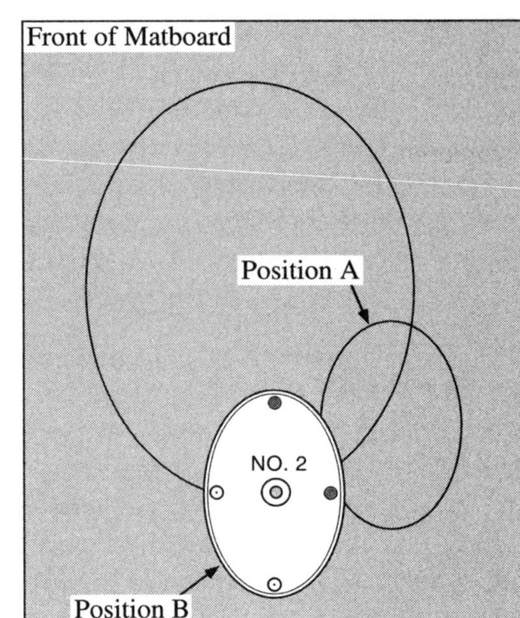

F

G

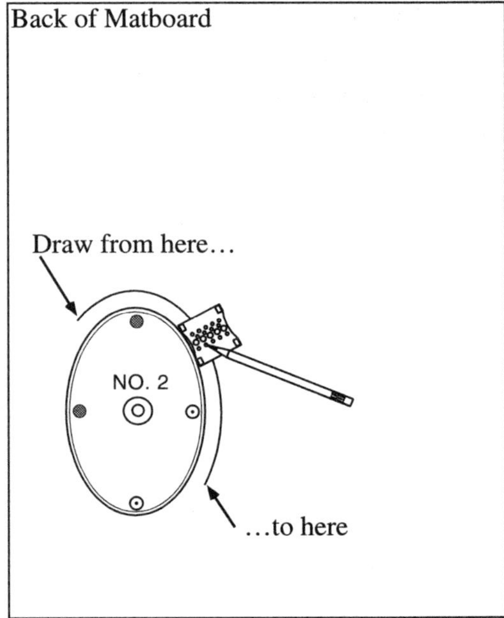

Design: Triple Ovals

9 **Still on back of matboard, replace the large #4 oval template so that the tacks are in the holes made in Step 1.** Pound tacks in. Lightly draw around the entire oval template (**Diagram H**). Remove the template.

CUTTING THE MAT

Focus on EACH cut to see: – where is the START – where is the STOP – <u>then</u>, and only then, cut.
For the cuts, in Steps 10, 12 and 13, start the cut 1/8" before the start line given and cut to 1/8" past the stop line given. You may find this too large of an overcut, but when learning this mat, it is better to overcut than to undercut.

To prevent breaking the tip of the blade off when starting the following cuts, (except Step 14), you need to:
1) Place the Model 30 about 1/16" away from the template.
2) Lower the blade into the matboard at the same angle it is sitting in the cutter, which will bring the two contact points of the Model 30 against the template.
Now you are ready to push the Model 30 around the template.

10 **On the back side of the matboard, secure the #2 template in the holes for Position B.** **Place the 3/8" spacer on the Alto's Model 30 cutter. Leave it in through Step 12. Start cutting at the bottom of the large oval template line and stop at the next line as shown (Diagram I).**

11 **The next cut starts at the line 1/2" from the end of the previous cut and stop 1/8" past the line drawn at the bottom of the first small oval as shown (Diagram J).** Remove template.

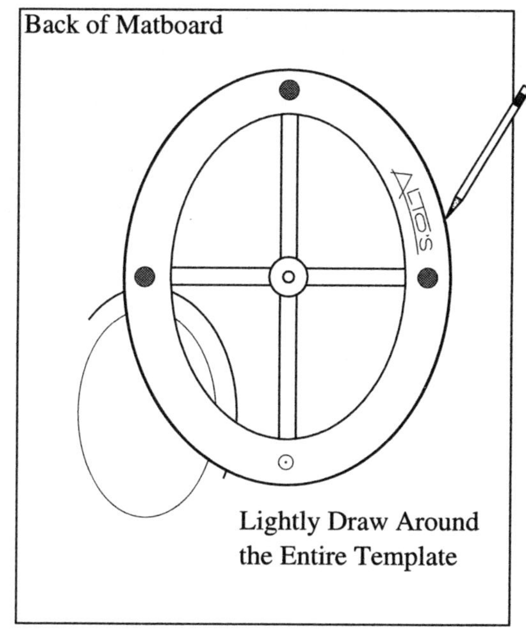

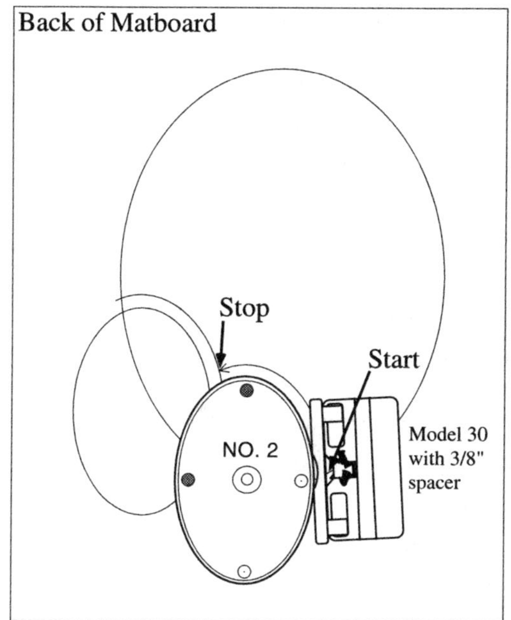

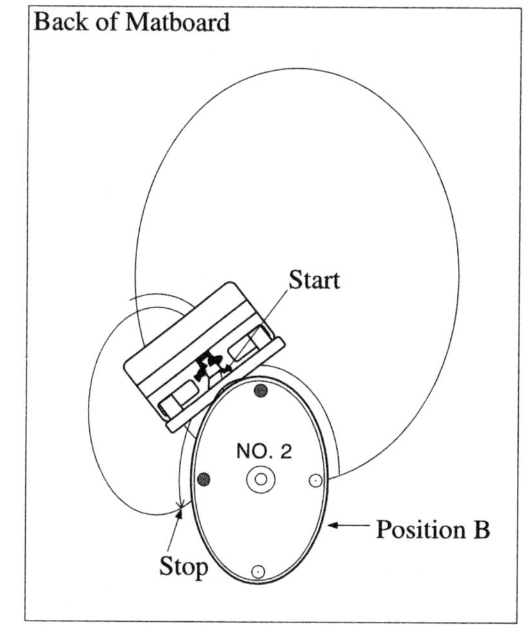

12 Place the template in the tack holes for Position A. Pound them in securely. **Cut, starting at the end of the cut in Step 10, and stopping at the pencil line at the left side of the large oval as shown (Diagram K).** Remove the template.

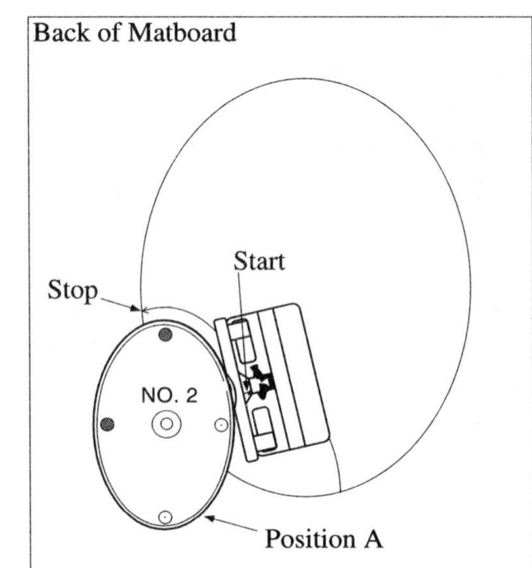

K

13 Flip matboard over so front is up and the small ovals are still toward the bottom. Remove the left tack of the small #2 template and replace it in the right side of the template. Remove 3/8" spacer from Model 30 cutter. Replace template in Position A and pound the tacks securely into the existing holes. **Cut, starting on the line at the lower right part of the Position B oval, and stopping at the line on top of the Position B oval as shown (Diagram L).** The window piece should come out with the template.

L

14 Replace window piece, and move the #2 template to Position B. Cut all the way around the oval so that the window piece falls out **(Diagram M).** Replace window piece.

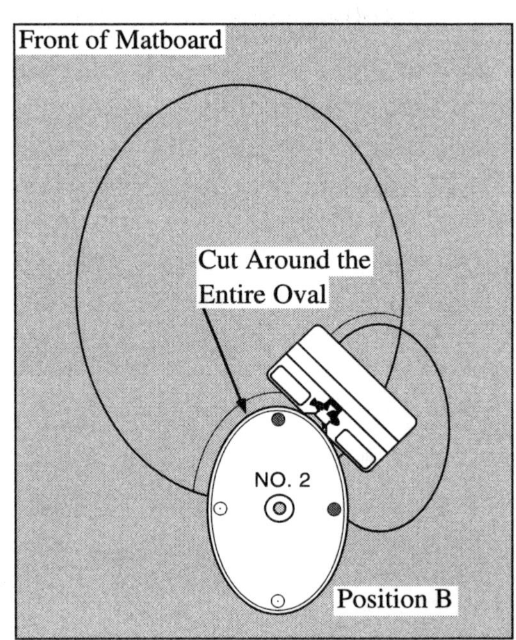

M

Design: Triple Ovals

15
Still on front of matboard, place #4 template in tack holes and pound in securely.
Cut around oval, starting at the line for Position A and ending at the line for Position B as shown **(Diagram N).** The last window piece should now fall out.

16
Using a plastic eraser, very gently erase all remaining pencil marks on front of mat so as to not discolor the mat. Too much pressure while erasing will cause a sheen on the mat surface.

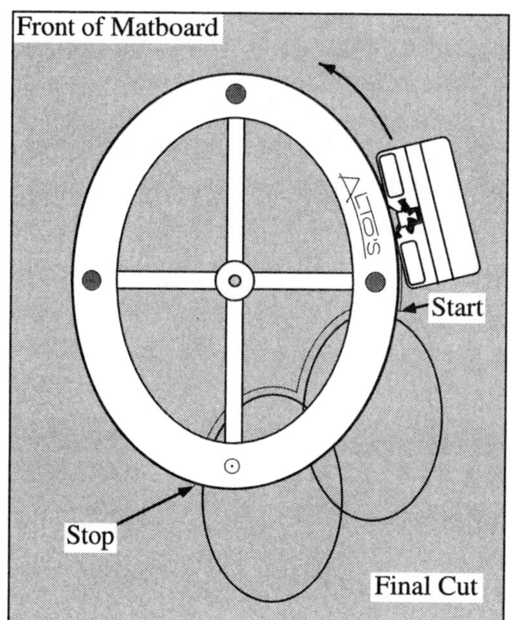

Now that you have successfully cut this mat design, experiment! Try a similar design using four openings or try the same design using #1 and #3 oval templates.

Any photos used in Position A or B of this design will have to be carefully trimmed to fit the shape of the mat.

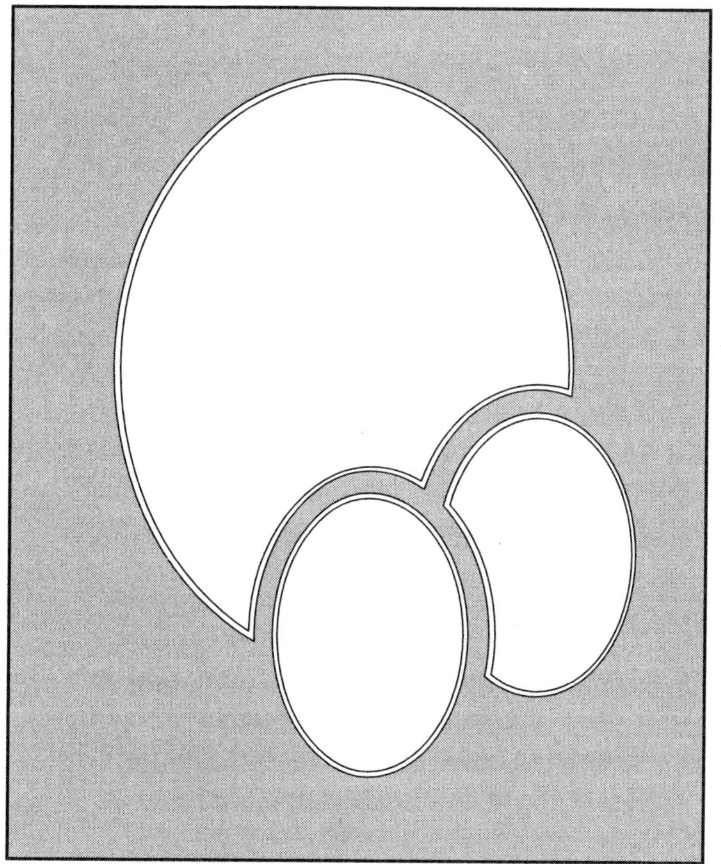

Cut–Out Accent

*T*his classic, elegant mat requires some careful cutting and gluing, but is quick and easy when following these steps one at a time.

Tools and materials needed

- Alto's 4501 or 4505 Mat Cutting System
- Two pieces of 11" x 14" matboard in complementary colors. The pieces of matboard must be exactly the same size
- Sharp blades
- Sharp pencil
- Non–abrasive eraser which won't mark or discolor the colored side of your matboard (test it on a scrap piece first)
- Double–stick tape
- Acid–free white glue
- 45°–45°–90° triangle

1 Set the dimensioning system at 3" and draw lines on all four sides of the back of the bottom mat **(Diagram A)**. Cut all four sides, so that the window piece falls out. Set this mat aside. The rest of the steps refer to the piece of matboard which will be your top mat.

2 Set the system at 2-3/4" and repeat all of Step 1 on the back of your top mat.

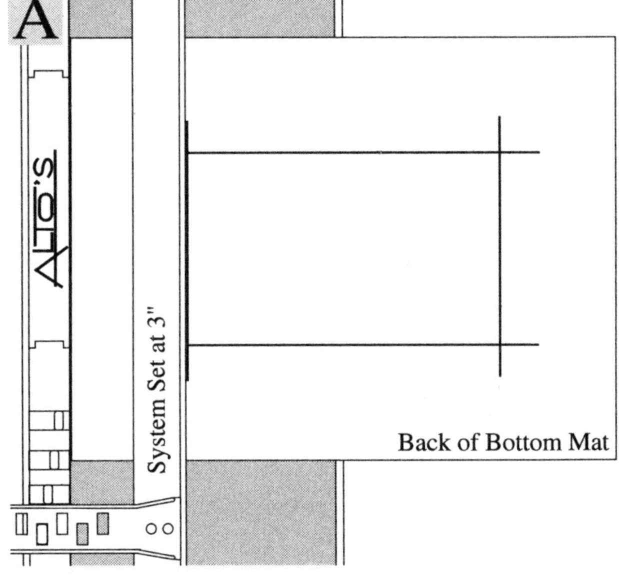

3 Leaving the top mat in the system, set the window piece aside and change the system to 2". Draw four more lines, one on each side of the back of the mat. Replace the window piece and cut all four sides, so that the new window piece falls out **(Diagram B)**. You now have three rectangles.

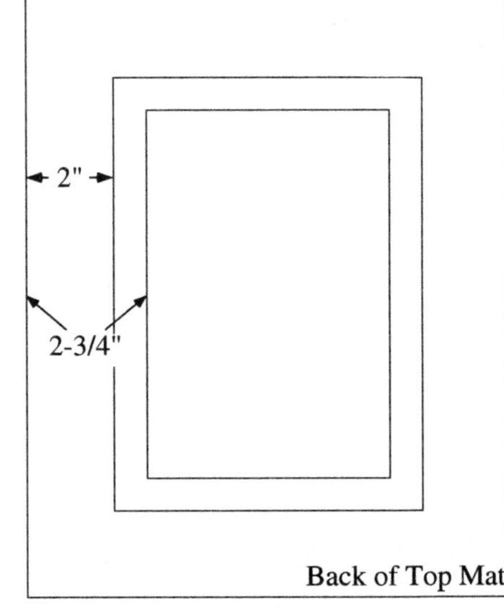

Design: Cut–Out Accent

4 **Place the largest, outside rectangle in the system, with the front side up.** Set the system at 1-3/4" and place the hypotenuse (the long side) of your triangle against the straightedge of your Alto's Mat Cutting System as shown (**Diagram C**). Draw a short line on the front of the mat from the inside corner of the mat to the straightedge (**Diagram C**). Repeat for the remaining corners.

5 **Replace both window pieces in the mat and place it in the system, front side up.**

6 **With the system still at 1-3/4", cut one side of the mat, using the short angled lines you drew in Step 4 as start/stop references (Diagram D).** This means that you sink the tip of the blade on the angled line closest to you, and cut until the silver line on the cutter is above the angled line farthest from you. Repeat for the remaining sides of the mat. *Using a soft, damp cloth, carefully clean the bottom of the Model 45 cutter between cuts to avoid smudging the pencil marks on the front of the mat.* The same two window pieces will fall out as before, but the window you just cut will not, because the corners are still attached.

7 **From the back of the mat, carefully insert a very sharp razor blade or Model 45 blade into one of the cuts you just made (at the same 45 degree angle). Gently slice through the last bit of matboard at the corner,** where it is still attached (**Diagram E**). Do not overcut. Repeat this for all four corners.
NOTE: It will take two of these cuts to release each corner of the mat, so you will make a total of eight cuts. The new piece should now fall out.

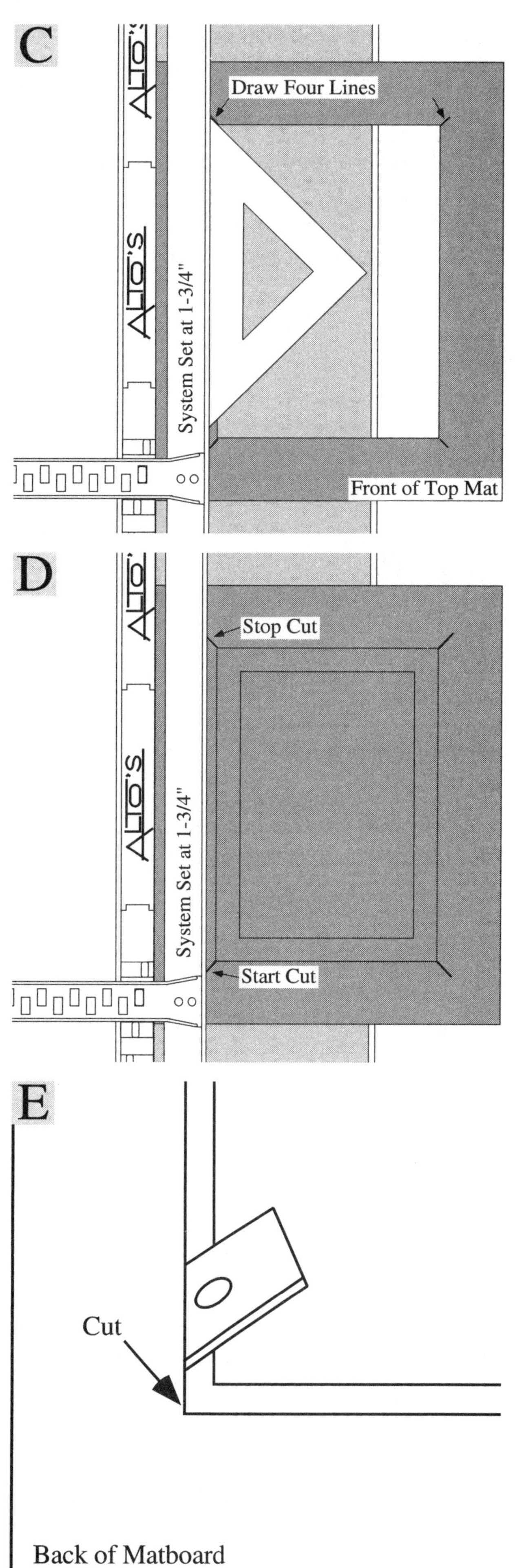

8 **Gently erase all pencil lines on the front of the mat.** Apply double stick tape to the back of the outside piece of your top mat.

9 **Carefully adhere it to the front side of the liner mat you cut in Step 1.** To make sure they are perfectly aligned, do this while looking straight down on them, not from an angle (**Diagram F**).

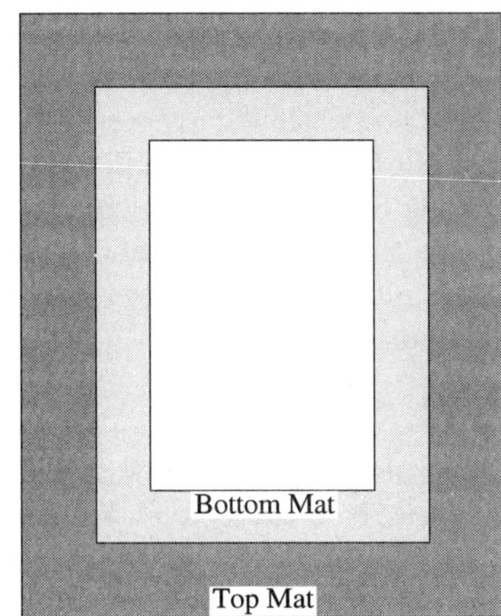

10 **Apply acid–free white glue <u>sparingly</u> to the back of the cut–out accent piece of the top mat.** Carefully adhere it to the front of the now double mat as shown (**Diagram G**), again looking straight down on the mats while aligning to insure accuracy. See detail for cross–section view of assembled mat.

G

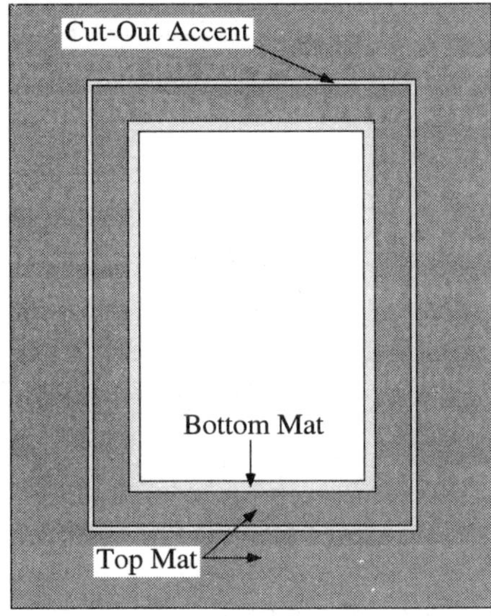

Detail

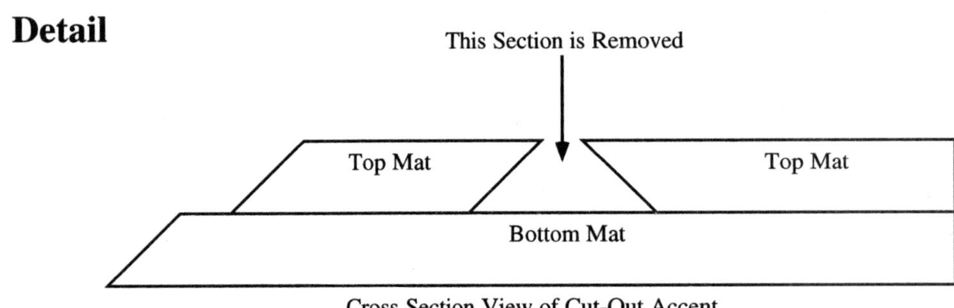

Design: Cut–Out Accent

Panoramic View

Focus on EACH cut to see: – where is the START – where is the STOP – then, and only then, cut.

This mat is perfect for framing panoramic scenes. It gives the effect of looking out through windows onto a landscape. Obviously, it is not for all applications as it covers a lot of the art piece. Use the title bar for the name of the place, if desired.

NOTE: The following instructions are a simplified, single mat version, of this mat shown on the cover. This mat is not for beginners. If you are a beginner, practice first on simpler designs and mats with step corners (see 4501 and 4505 Mat Cutting System Instructions, p. 15). Practice this design on a scrap piece of matboard first. Do all drawing and cutting on the back of the mat. As always, be sure to use a sharp blade when cutting your mats.

   Materials: Alto's 4501 or 4505 Mat Cutting System, a sharp pencil for accurate drawing, double–stick tape, and several 11" x 14" pieces of matboard, a couple for practice and one for the final mat.

LAY OUT THE OVERALL WINDOW SIZES

1 **Preparation: On the back of your matboard, label one of the long sides "Top", and the other one "Bottom".** Mark the short sides "Side 1" and "Side 2".

2 **Set the dimensioning system at 1-3/4", and on the back of the matboard draw reference lines on the sides and at the top as shown (Diagram A).**

3 **Set the system at 4-1/4".** Draw the reference line as shown (**Diagram A**).

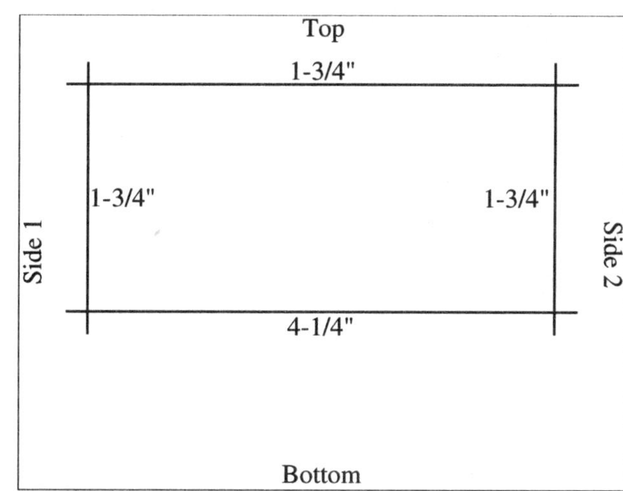

DRAWING REFERENCE LINES FOR THE TITLE BLOCK

4 **Move the system to 1-3/4", place the bottom against the stops.** Draw a reference line (**Diagram B**).

5 **Without moving the mat, set the system at 3".** Draw the upper reference line (**Diagram B**).

6 **Move the system to 4-1/4".** For these two reference lines place the sides against the stops. Draw the reference lines (**Diagram B**).

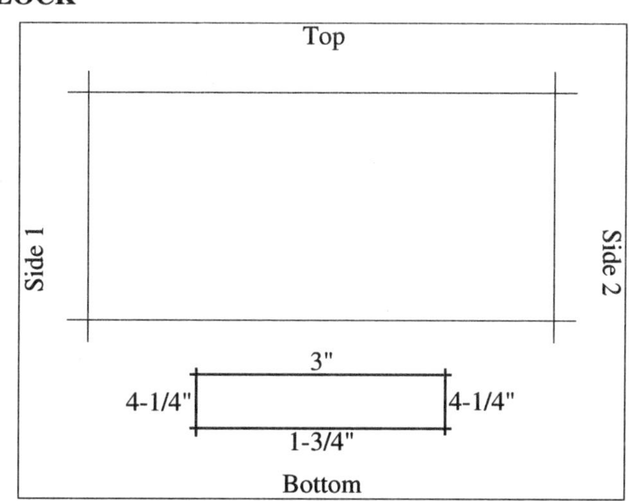

DRAWING THE REMAINING REFERENCE LINES FOR THE PANORAMIC WINDOWS

7 **Set the system at 3-1/2".** Place the sides, in turn, against the stops. Draw the reference lines **(Diagram C)**.

8 **Set the system at 4-1/2".** Place the sides, in turn, against the stops. Draw the reference lines **(Diagram C)**.

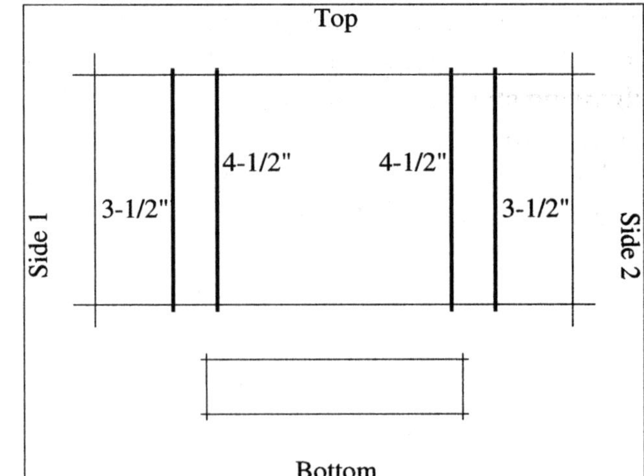

LAY OUT THE UPPER CORNER DESIGNS

Diagram D shows what the corner stepped reference lines **will look like** after you have completed Steps 9, 10, 11 and 12. Corners A and B have the same dimensions, except turned around **(Diagram D)**.

9 **Place "Side 1" against the stops and set the system at 3-1/2" on the A–C line.** Move the system 1/4" smaller to 3-1/4" and draw a short reference line as illustrated. Move the system 1/4" smaller (down two posts) to 3" and draw two short reference lines, one as before across the upper horizontal line, and another short line in the middle of the window as illustrated. Move the system 1/4" smaller to 2-3/4" and draw your fourth short reference line **(Diagram E)**.

10 **With "Side 1" still against the stops and set the system at 4-1/2" on the B–D line and repeat Step 9, except you are moving the Cutting Guide away from the side (Diagram E). (4-3/4", 5", and 5-1/4").**

11 **Place "Side 2" against the stops and repeat Steps 9 and 10 on the other side.**

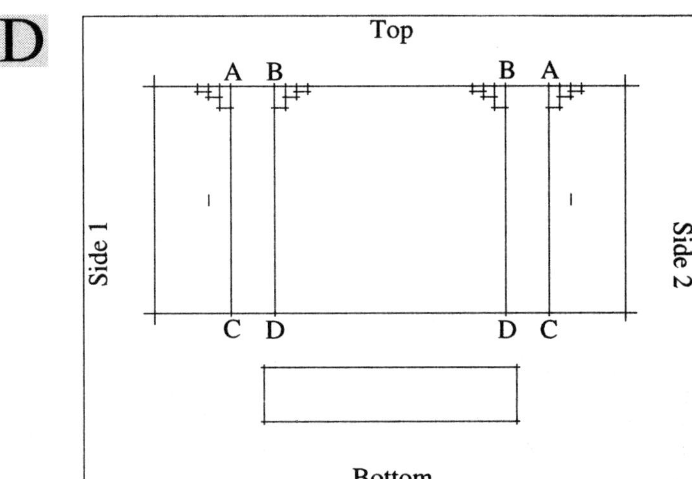

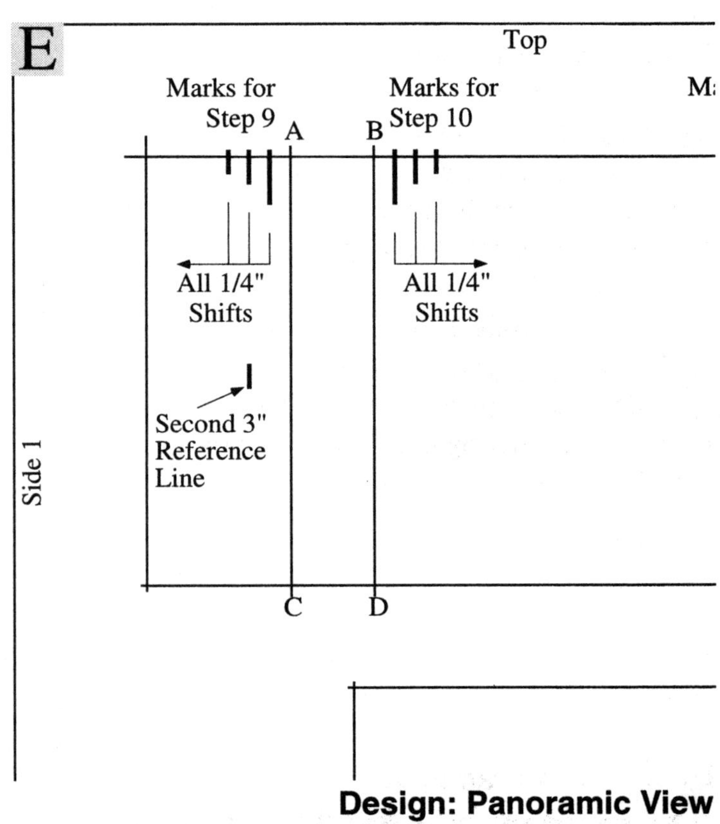

Design: Panoramic View

12
Place the Top edge against the stops. Set the system on the A–B line at 1-3/4". Repeat the same procedure of moving the system away from the stops, and drawing short reference lines. Resetting the system from 1-3/4" out 1/8" (up one post) to 1-7/8", then again 1/8" to 2", finally 1/4" (up two posts) to 2-1/4" (**Diagram F**).

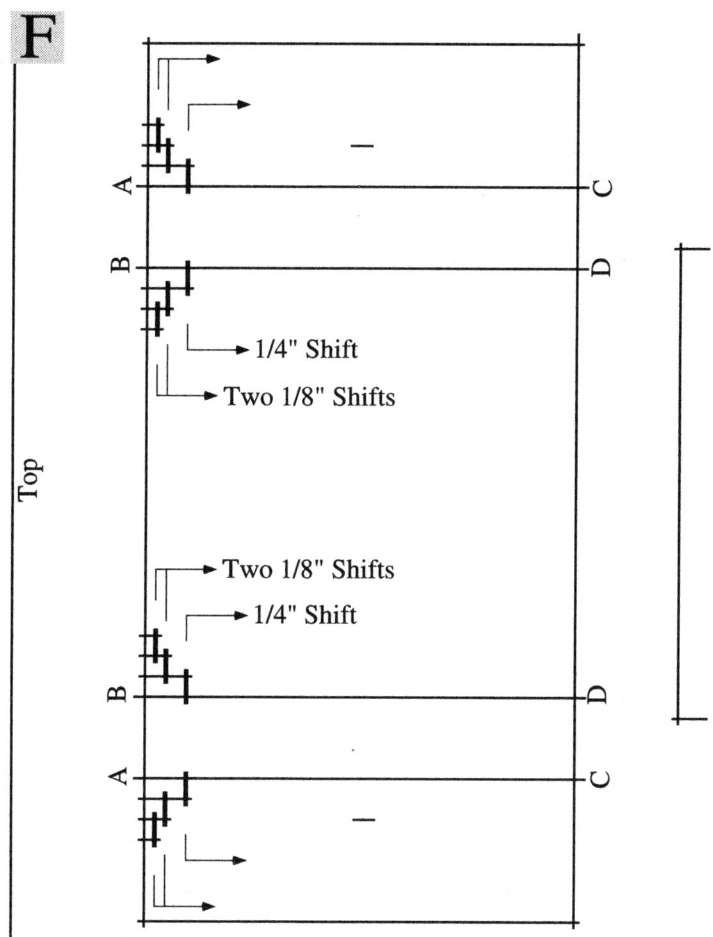

LAY OUT THE LOWER CORNER DESIGNS

13
Place "Side 1" against the stops and set the system at 3-1/2" on the A–C line. Move the system 1/4" smaller to 3-1/4" and draw a short reference line as illustrated. Move the system smaller 1/2" (same post, new hole) towards the stops to 2-3/4" and draw a short reference line. Move the system 1/4" smaller to 2-1/2" and draw two short reference lines, one as before across the upper horizontal line, and another short line in the middle of the window as illustrated (**Diagram G**).

14
With "Side 1" still against the stops and the system set at 4-1/2" on the B–D line and repeat Step 12, except you are moving the Cutting Guide away from the side (**Diagram G**). (4-3/4", 5-1/4", and 5-1/2").

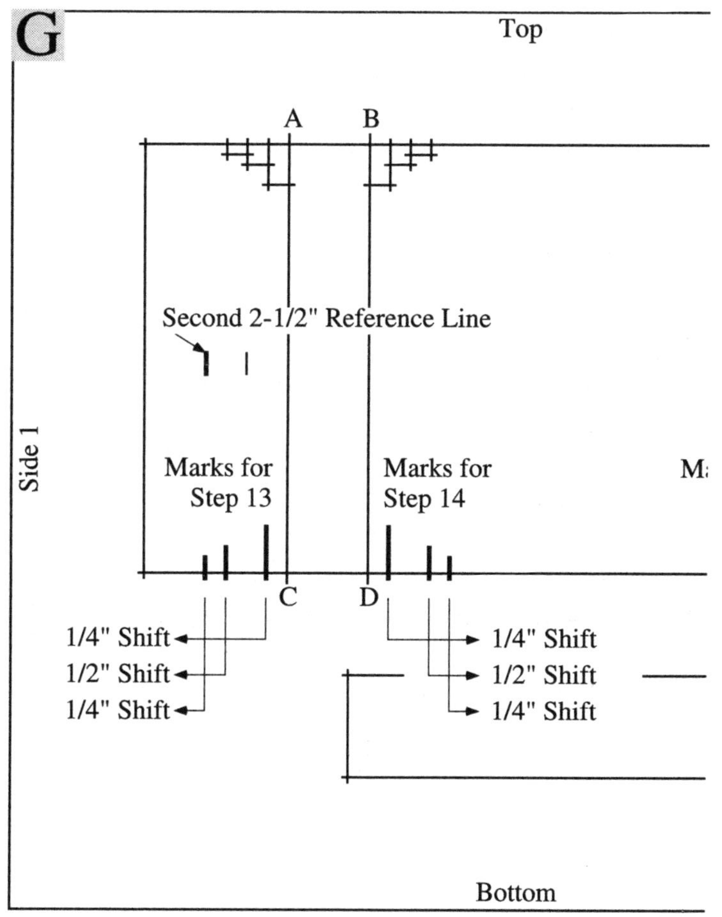

15
Place "Side 2" against the stops and repeat Steps 13 and 14 on the other side.

16
Place the Bottom edge against the stops. Set the system on the C–D line at 4-1/4". Repeat the same procedure of moving the system away from the stops, and drawing short reference lines. Resetting the system from 4-1/4" out 1/8" (one post) to 4-3/8", then again 1/8" to 4-1/2", finally another 1/4" (two posts) to 4-3/4" **(Diagram H)**.

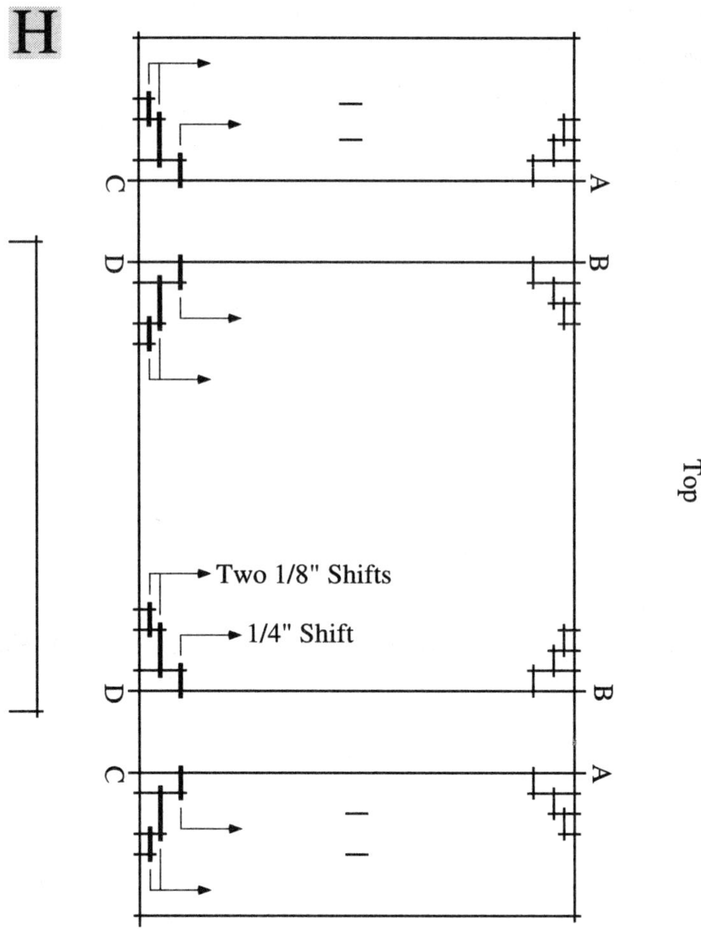

LAY OUT THE BOTTOM WINDOW CORNER DESIGNS

17
Place "Side 1" against the stops and put the system at 4-3/4". Draw two reference lines as shown **(Diagram I)**. Rotate the mat 180° to "Side 2" and draw two more short reference lines **(Diagram I)**.

18
Place the "Bottom" against the stops and set the system at 1-7/8". Draw two reference lines as shown **(Diagram J)**.

19
Set the system at 2-7/8". Draw two reference lines as shown **(Diagram J)**.

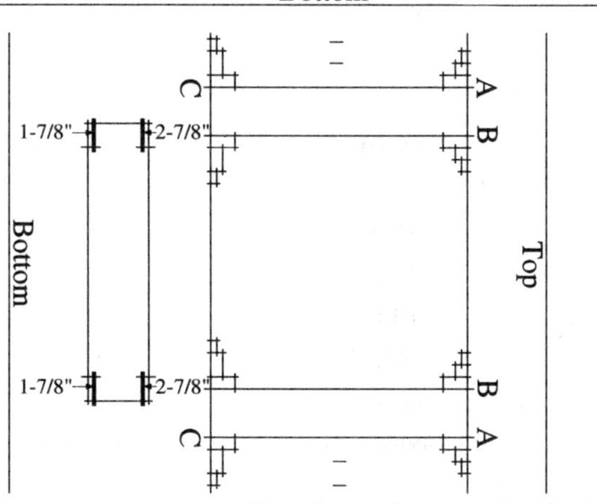

Design: Panoramic View

PREPARATION FOR CUTTING THE EDGES

20 Carefully erase excess lines, especially those between the windows and any lines in the corners that are not used for start/stop reference lines (Diagram K).

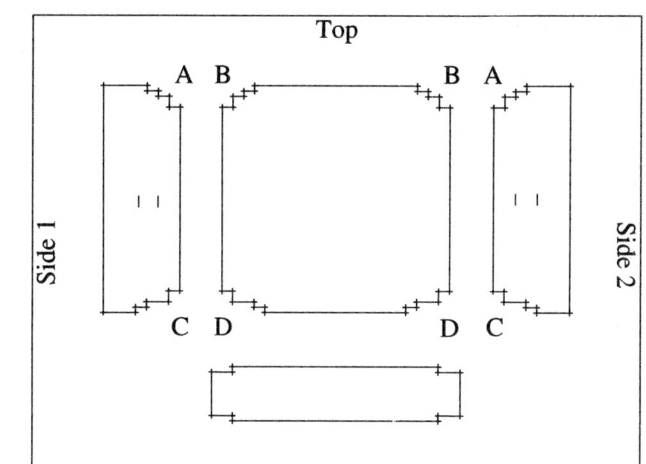

CUTTING THE MAT

If you are familiar with cutting stepped corners and Far–Cuts*, go ahead and cut this mat, remembering to *cut all the short cuts first and then the long cuts for each window*.

NOTE: It is very important, when cutting this mat, to pay close attention to start/stop reference lines. Some lines on this design are drawn with 1/8" increments. Because of this, you may occasionally be cutting directly on a pencil line. Don't be confused by this; *always use the reference lines coming from the pencil line that the straight edge is lined up on, not the one running parallel to your blade.*

21 The first several cuts for this mat will be Far–Cuts on both "Side" windows. Recall that these are done by setting the system at 5" and sliding the matboard over the stops and under the straight edge as shown **(Diagram L)**. You then move the mat to align it with the pencil lines you wish to cut. Seven Far–Cuts will be made on "Side 2" with "Side 1" <u>over</u> the stops. *For the first and fourth Far–Cuts you will line up the stepped reference line and the short reference line marked in the middle of the side window opening as a second reference mark to make sure the cut is parallel to the other cuts.* The seventh cut is the inside edge of the "Side 2" window. Turn the mat 180° and repeat for "Side 1" with "Side 2" over the stops.

*Far–Cuts are cuts made farther, or beyond, the standard reach[1] of the dimensioning system. For many of you this concept will not become clear until you actually do it. For this Panoramic View mat, there are <u>seventeen</u> Far–Cuts. Seven on "Side 2," seven on "Side 1," and three in the title block.

[1] The standard reach of the 4501 dimensioning system is 6". The 4505 dimension system will reach out to 8".

Design: Panoramic View

22 Lift the mat edge marked "Top" over the stops and cut three Far–Cuts in the title block (Diagram M).

Steps 23 – 27 involve selecting lines that <u>can</u> be reached by the Cutting Guide (Straightedge).

23 Place "Side 1" against the stops and set the system near the "B" and "D" line. **These ten cuts will be in both the center window and the title block.** Move the system on the far line. *In Diagram N the "1st Cut" (5-1/2" setting) starts on the start reference line and cuts into the window about a half an inch past the next horizontal line. The "3rd Cut" starts in the window about a half an inch before the start reference line and stops on the stop reference line* (Diagram N).

24 Turn the matboard 180° so "Side 2" is against the stops and repeat Step 22 cutting ten more cuts (No Diagram).

25 Place the edge marked "Bottom" against the stops. Cut all of the lower cuts of the panoramic window and the short cuts of the title block, 4-3/4", 4-1/2", 4-3/8", & 1-7/8" (No Diagram).

26 Place the edge marked "Top" against the stops. Cut only the corner cuts of the panoramic windows, 2-1/4", 2", & 1-7/8" (No Diagram). Do not cut the top edges yet (1-3/4" setting).

27 Set the system at 1-3/4" for the remainder of the cuts. Place the "Bottom" against the stops. Cut the bottom edge of the title block. The title block window should fall out. Put the "Top" against the stops and cut the three edges of the panoramic windows. The center window should fall free. Put "Side 1" against the stops and cut. The "Side 1" window should fall out. Put "Side 2" against the stops and cut. The "Side 2" window should fall out (No Diagram).

28 Congratulate yourself (No Diagram).

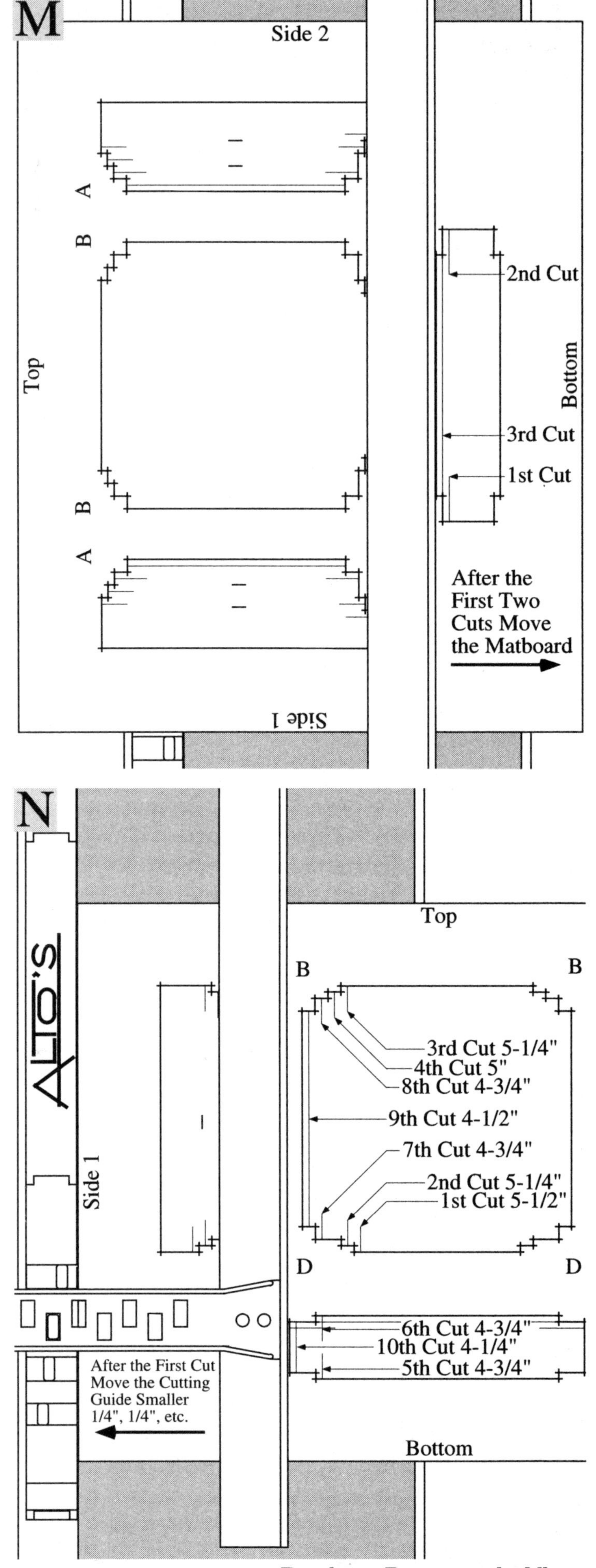

Design: Panoramic View

U**sing this mat design concept many interesting mats can be cut.** Try making a few of your own. You'd be surprised at how much fun it is.

Design: Panoramic View

Rectang–O

*T**his double mat is done in four stages.*
First, you'll lay out the bottom mat, then lay out the top mat, then you'll cut the arcs, then cut the circular windows, and lastly you'll be cutting the outer edges.

Tools and materials needed

- Alto's 4501 or 4505 Mat Cutting System
- Alto's Model 360 Circle Cutter
- Two pieces of 11" x 14" matboard exactly the same size
- Scrap piece of matboard as a cutting surface*
- Sharp blades
- Sharp pencil
- Non–abrasive eraser
- Double–stick tape
- Acid–free white glue

*When using the Model 360 try using a piece of 3/4" plywood <u>under</u> your cutting surface. 3/4" plywood is flat and holds the centering tack secure.

PREPARE THE MATBOARD

On the long side of one piece of matboard write "Top Mat." On the long side of the other piece of matboard write "Bottom Mat."

LAY OUT THE BOTTOM MAT

1 **Set the dimensioning system at 2-1/4" and draw reference lines on four sides of the mat (Diagram A).**

2 **Set the system at 4" and draw four short reference lines as illustrated (Diagram B).**

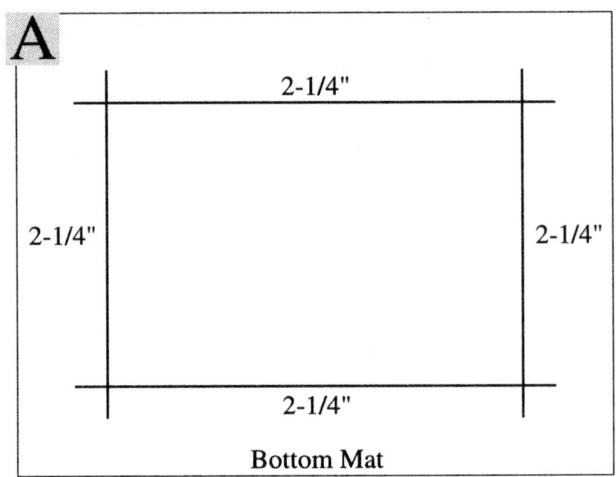

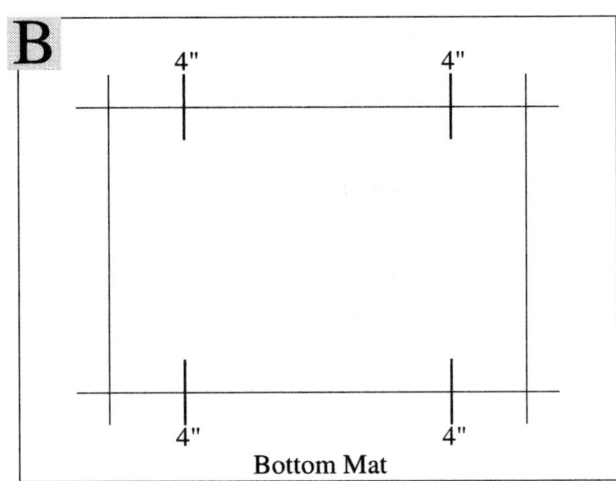

Design: Rectang–O

3 Draw an "x" of short lines in the center of the mat by laying a straightedge from corner to corner of the matboard (Diagram C).

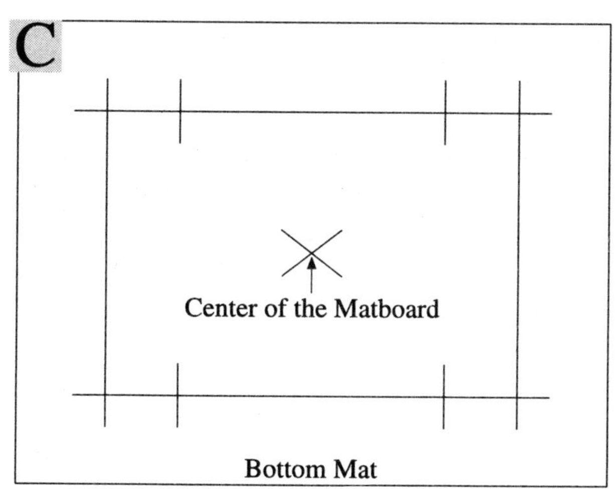

4 Push a tack through the mat at the center location (Diagram D).

NOTE: The layout for the window sizes and the arc sizes will be given when you are ready to cut the circular edges.

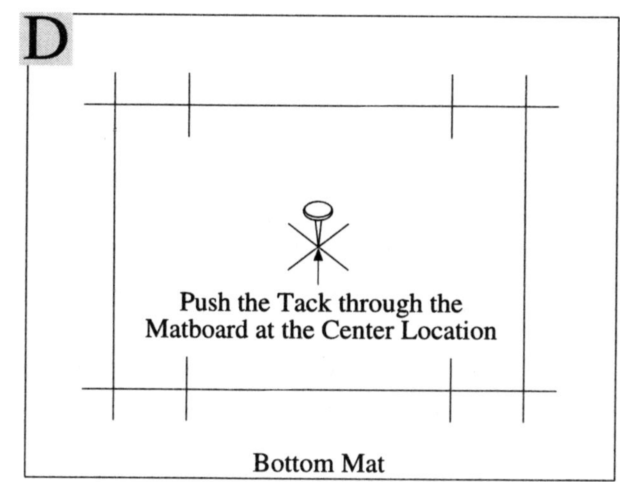

LAY OUT THE TOP MAT

5 Set the system at 2" and draw reference lines (Diagram E).

6 Set the system at 4-3/4" and draw four short reference lines (Diagram E).

7 Find the center as in Step 3 or align the bottom mat on the top mat and push the tack through both mats.

NOTE: You will use the same center hole for all circles and arcs.

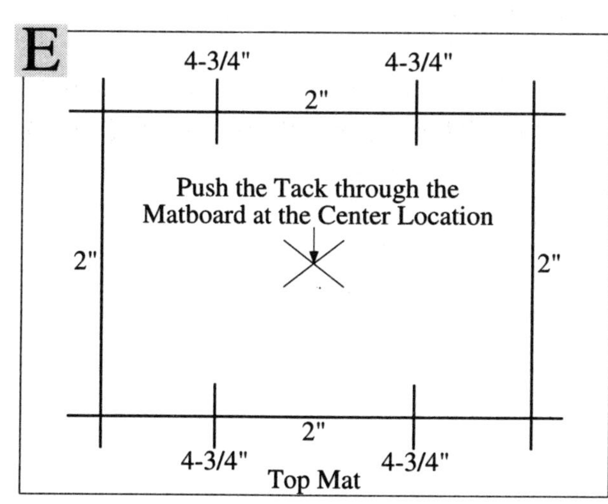

CUTING THE ARCS

8 **For the bottom mat set the Model 360 circle cutter at the 9" setting and insert the tack through the center tack hole in the mat.**
NOTE: Be especially careful to insert the tack exactly in the hole to insure accurate circles.

9 **a) Cut two arcs in the mat, one on each side. Start the point of the blade 1/16" before the vertical short reference line and cut around the arc to the next vertical reference line (Diagram F).**
b) Turn mat, leaving the Model 360 tack in place. Cut the second arc.

10 **Cut the two similar arcs in the top mat with the Model 360 set at 8-1/2" (Diagram F).**

CUTTING THE CIRCULAR WINDOWS

11 **The circle windows are cut from the *front side* of the mat.** For the top mat set the Model 360 at 7-1/2". Insert the tack through the center hole in the mat and cut the circle **(Diagram G).**
NOTE: Start the cut by lowering the blade slowly as you move the cutter forward.

12 **Cut a similar circle in the bottom mat with the Model 360 set at 7" (Diagram G).**

CUTTING THE OUTER EDGES

13 **For the bottom mat, set the system at 2-1/4".** Cut remaining edges on all four sides. Start on the reference lines closest to you and cut to the reference lines furthest from you **(Diagram H).**

14 **For the top mat, set the system at 2" and cut the remaining edges as you did in Step 13 (Diagram H).**

15 **Carefully align the top and bottom mats.** Adhere them together with double–stick tape **(Diagram I).**

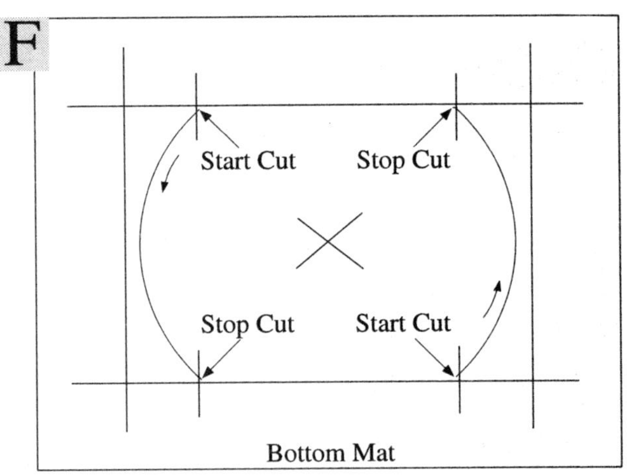

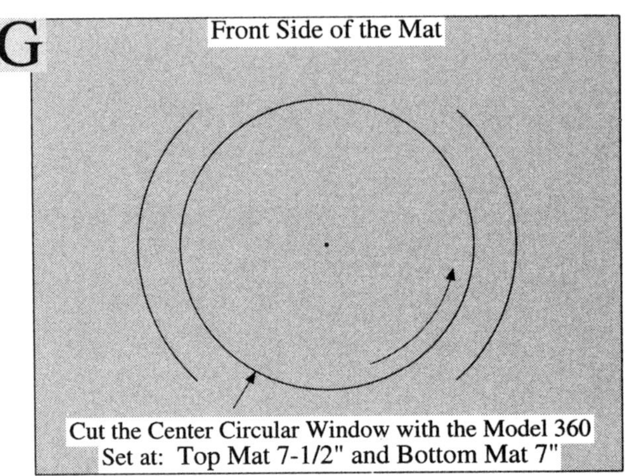

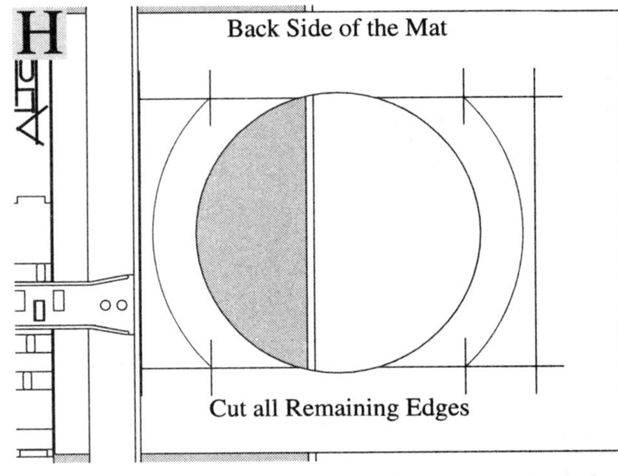

Design: Rectang–O

Octagon with Dovetail Edges

The lay out of the top mat of this double mat requires many lines at varying angles. Proceed slowly, being diligent as to where you are at in the process.

Tools and materials needed
- Alto's 4501 or 4505 Mat Cutting System
- Two pieces of 11" x 11" matboard exactly the same size
- Sharp blade
- Sharp pencil
- Double–stick tape
- 45°–45°–90° triangle
- Ruler or straightedge

For ease of layout, we will be working with a square format. Once you have cut this mat design, it will be easy to transfer the design to a rectangular format if needed.

LAY OUT AND CUT THE BOTTOM MAT

1 **Set the dimensioning system at 2-3/4".** Draw four reference lines around the mat. Label these lines "A" **(Diagram A)**.

2 **Set the system at 4-1/2".** Draw eight short lines across lines "A", as illustrated. Label these lines "B" **(Diagram B)**.

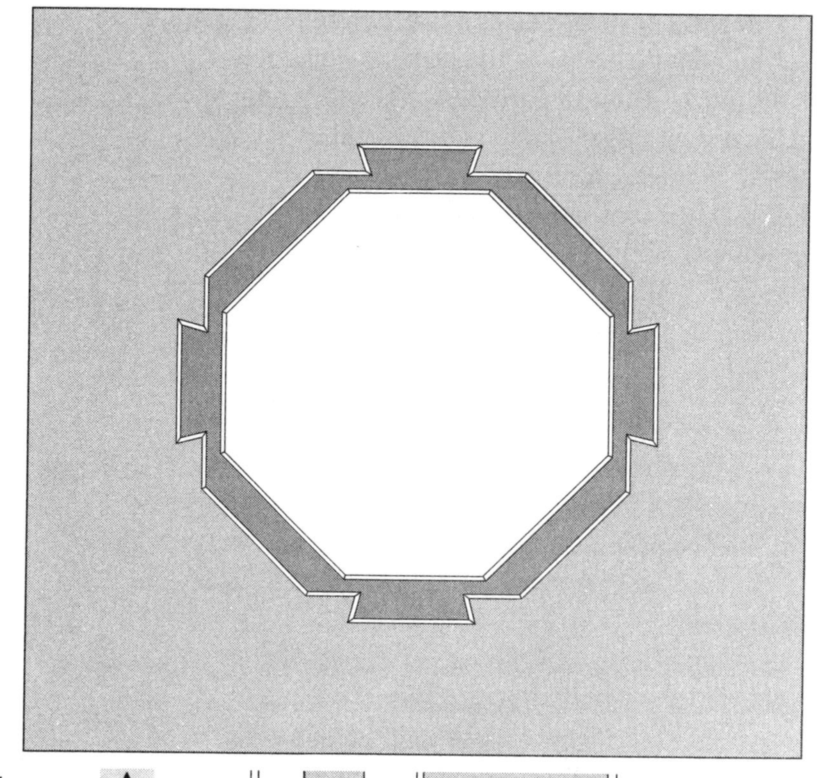

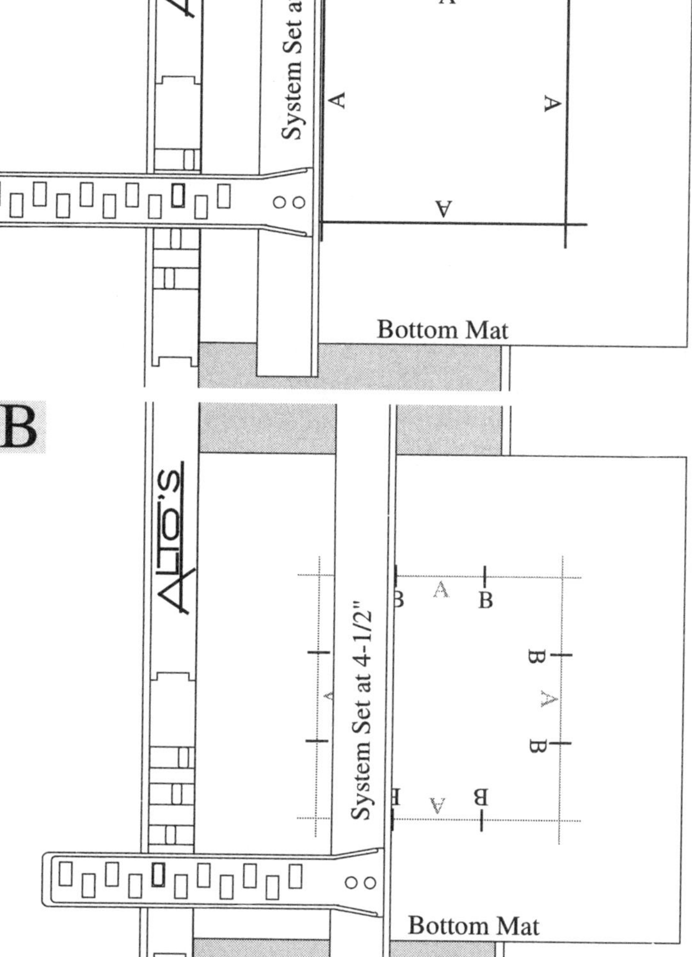

3 **Set the system at 5-1/2".** Place the triangle against the stops as illustrated. Place the mat under the cutting guide against the triangle. Adjust the mat so that the cutting guide lines up with the intersections of lines "A" and "B." Draw a line that intersects the short lines "B", as shown. Repeat for each corner. Label these lines "C" **(Diagram C)**.

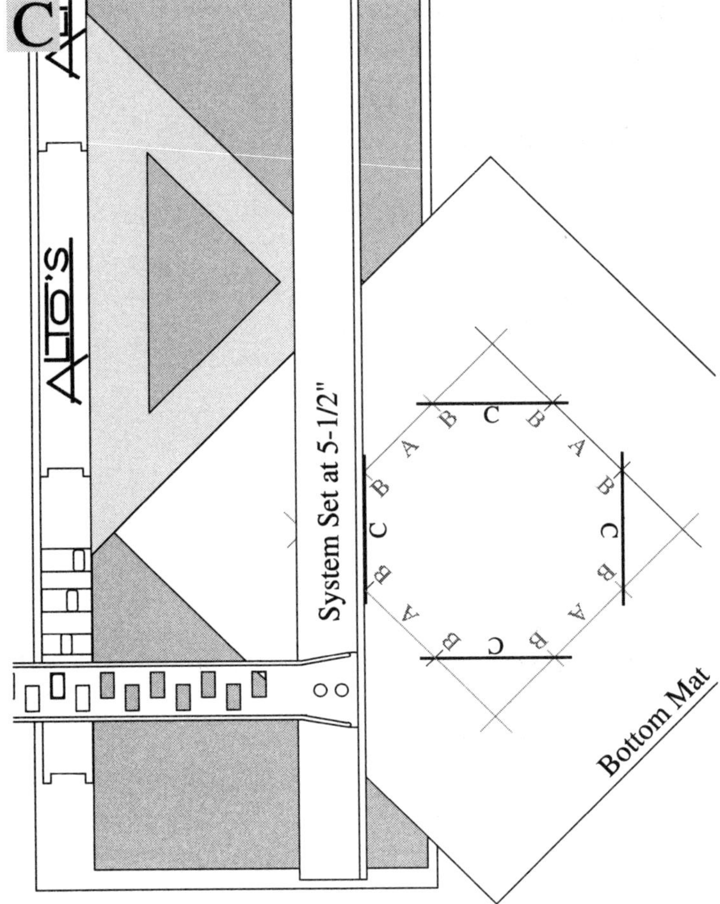

4 **Make the diagonal cuts.** Place mat so that the cutting guide is on one of the lines drawn in Step 3. Make the diagonal cut. Begin your cut slightly before and end it slightly after the reference lines "B" **(Diagram D)**. Repeat for the remaining corners.

5 **Set the system at 2-3/4" and make the remaining cuts (No Diagram).** The octagon–shaped window should now fall out. Set the bottom mat aside.

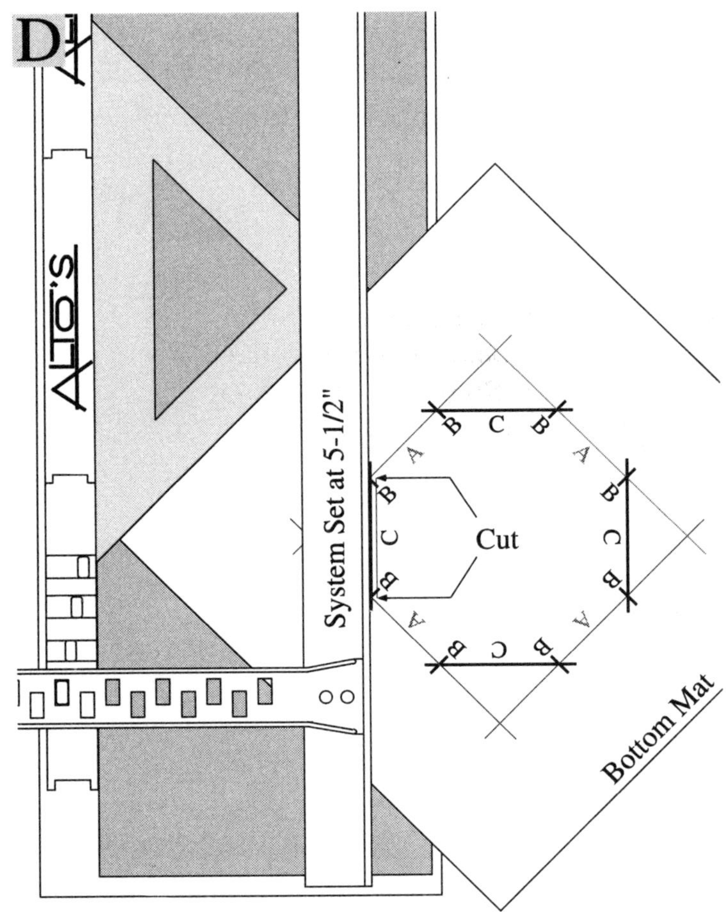

Design: Octagon with Dovetail Edges

LAY OUT AND CUT THE TOP MAT

6 **Set the system at 2-1/2".** Draw four
reference lines as shown. Label these
lines "D" (**Diagram E**).

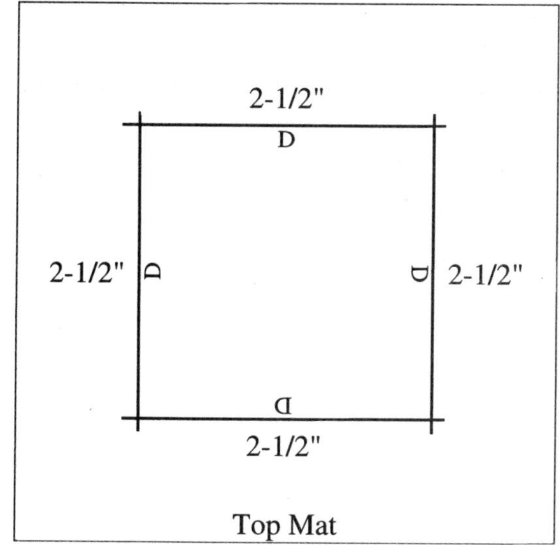

7 **Set the system at 4".** Draw eight short
reference lines across lines "D" as shown.
Label these lines "E" (**Diagram F**).

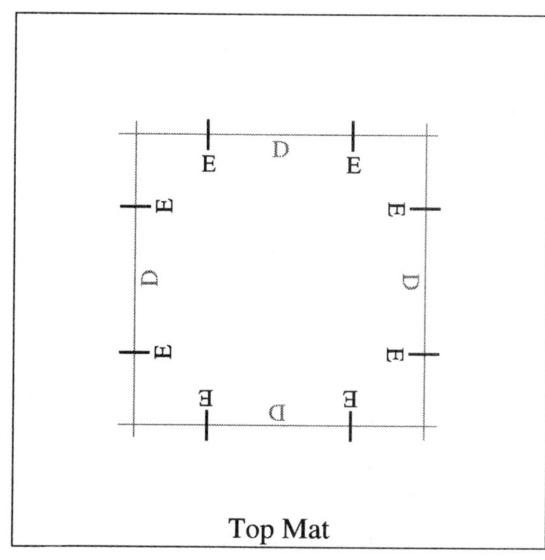

8 Using your triangle and straightedge,
draw a diagonal reference line at each
corner just like Step 3, as illustrated.
Label these lines "F" (**Diagram G**).

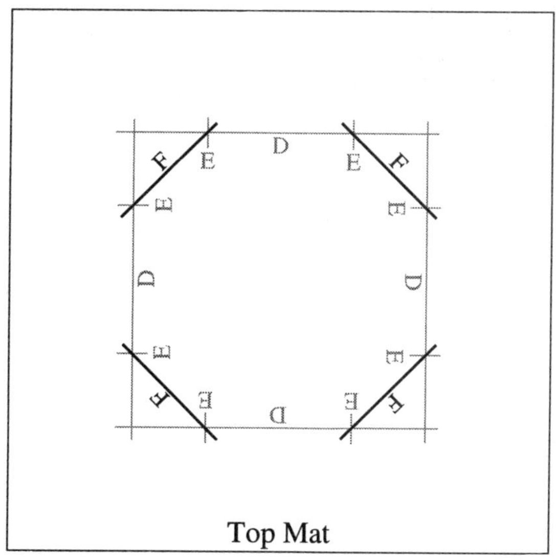

Design: Octagon with Dovetail Edges

9 Set the system at 2-1/8". Draw four reference lines as shown. Label these lines "G" (**Diagram H**).

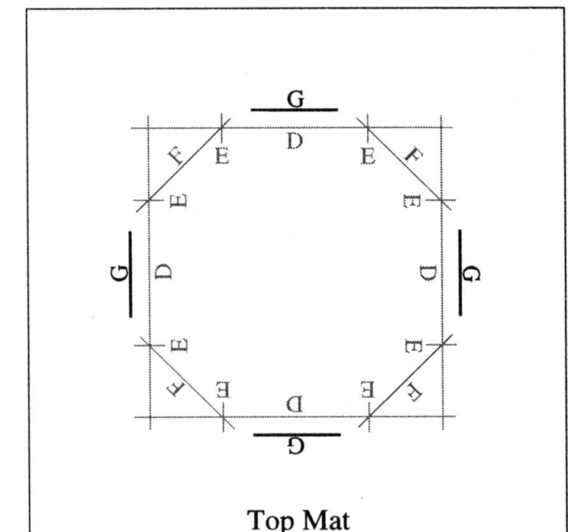

10 Set the system at 4-5/8". Draw eight short reference lines across lines "G" as illustrated. Label these lines "H" (**Diagram I**).

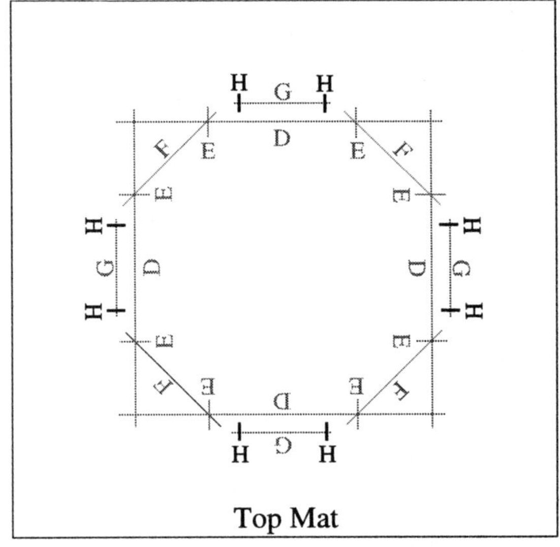

11 Place your straightedge across the mat so that it connects two opposing intersections of lines "H" and "G" as shown. Draw a reference line at each end of the straightedge toward the center of the mat. Repeat for other sides, eight lines total. Label these lines "I" (**Diagram J**).

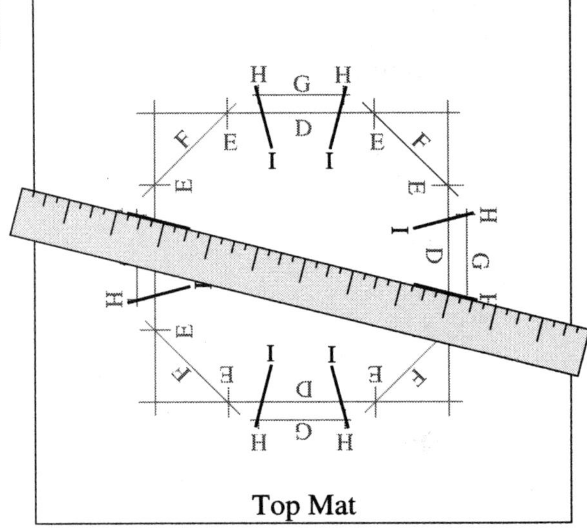

   Design: Octagon with Dovetail Edges

12 Place the straightedge on two opposing reference lines "I", as shown.

NOTE: Since the mat isn't butted against the stops, firmly press on the cutting guide with your left hand to prevent the mat from slipping when you cut. Make *one* cut from line "G" toward the center of the mat **(Diagram K)**. The Model 45 should be on the "G" side of line "I" and not the "E" side.

Do not cut all the way across the mat. To do so will cut part of the bevel the wrong way.

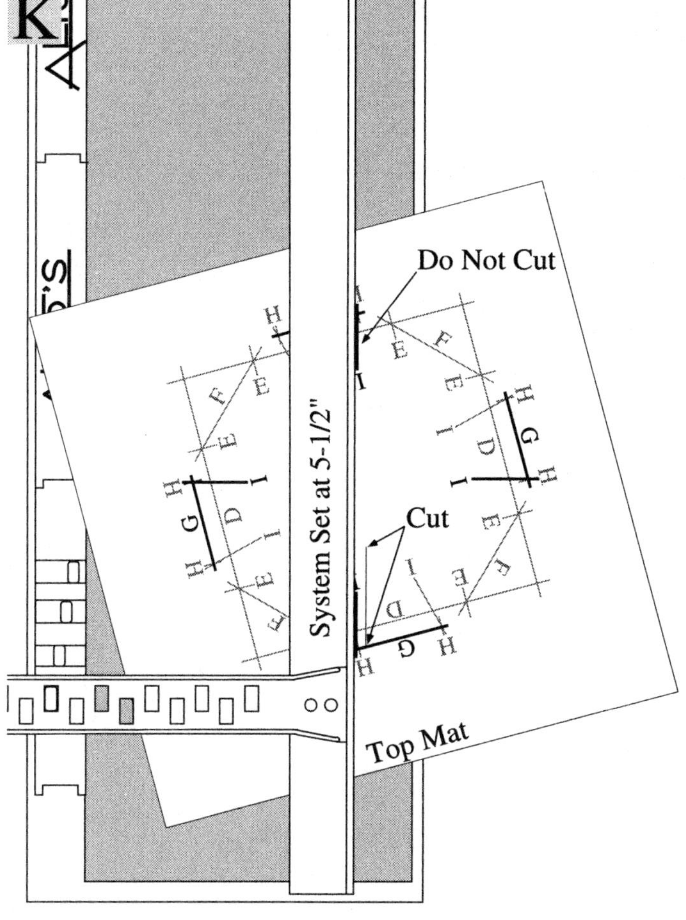

13 Rotate the mat to the left, to the next set of reference lines. Make one cut, from the center of the window, to line "G" **(Diagram L)**. Continue around the mat making these alternating cuts, eight total.

14 Using the cutting technique in Step 4, make the four diagonal cuts along the line labeled "F" (No Diagram).

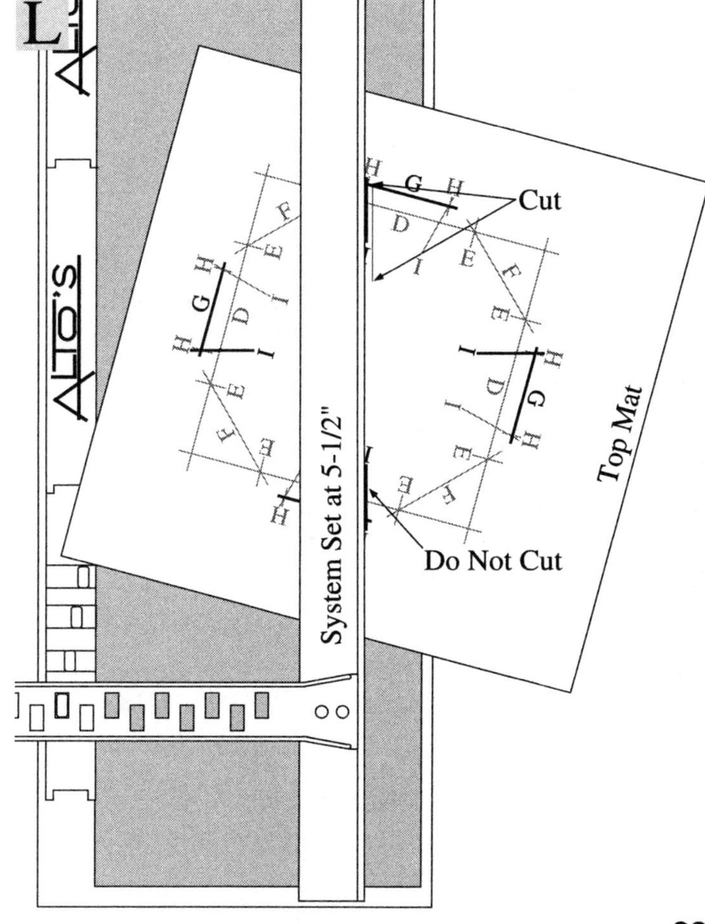

15 Set the system at 2-1/8". Make four cuts using lines "H" as the start/stop references (**Diagram M**).

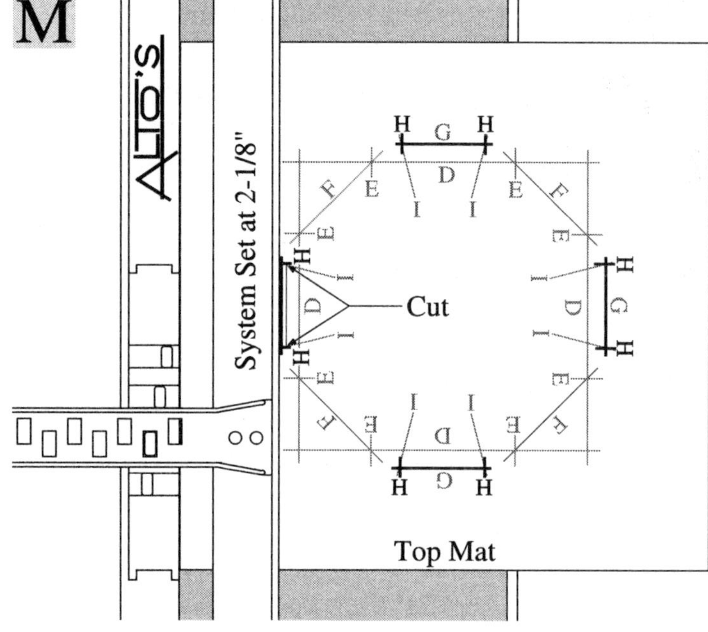

16 Set the system at 2-1/2". Make the four remaining cuts. Begin your cuts just before, and end them just after reference lines "E". On each side, make one continuous cut, to ensure that the acute angles are cut cleanly (**Diagram N**).

17 The octagon–with–dovetail shaped window should now fall out. If not, use a sharp blade to carefully finish any unfinished cuts.

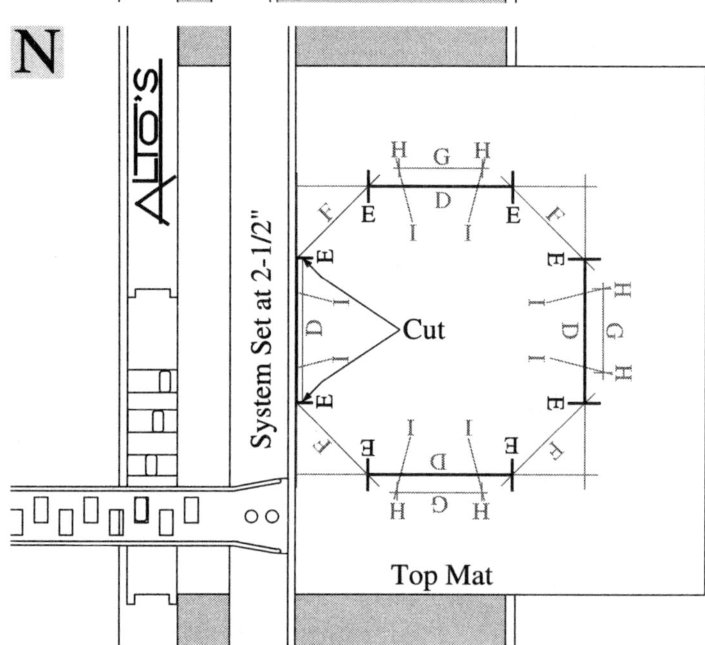

18 Carefully align and join the two mats together with double–stick tape (**Diagram O**).

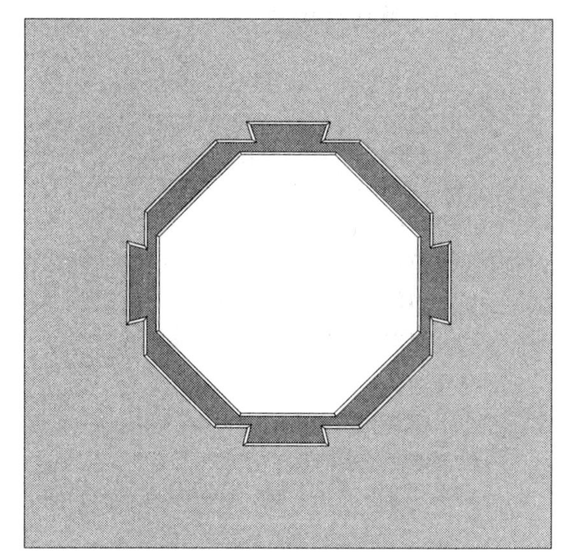

　　　　Design: Octagon with Dovetail Edges

Circular Window with Scalloped Border

*W*ith this mat you will be using your Alto's Model 360 to lay out and cut this unique mat design.

Tools and materials needed
- Alto's Model 360 Circle Cutter
- Two pieces of 10" x 10" matboard and one piece of 11" x 14" matboard all in contrasting colors
- Scrap piece of matboard as a cutting surface*
- Sharp blade
- Sharp pencil
- Double–stick tape
- Acid–free white glue
- Ruler

*When using the Model 360 try using a piece of 3/4" plywood <u>under</u> your cutting surface. 3/4" plywood is flat and holds the centering tack secure.

1 **On the back of one of the 10" x 10" pieces, find the center of the mat by placing your ruler from corner to corner, and drawing an "X" in the center of the matboard.** Next, align the two 10" x 10" pieces, one on top of the other, and poke the tack from the Model 360 through the center of the "X", making sure that you put a hole through both pieces of matboard (**Diagram A**).

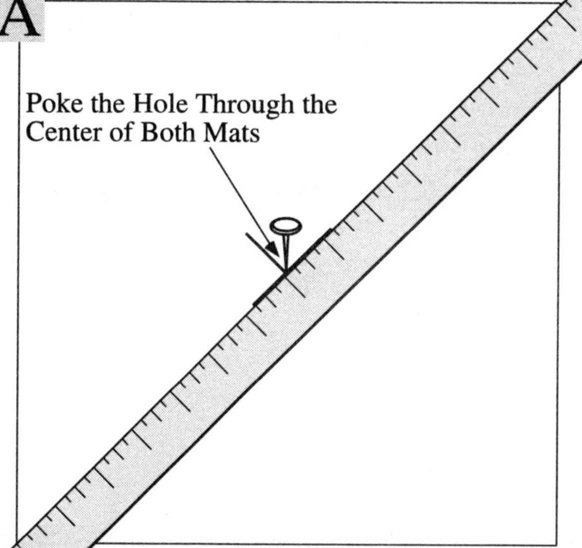

TOP MAT

2 **Place the tack for the Model 360 in the 30" hole of the Model 360 extension.** Then place the tack, with extension, through the hole in the top matboard from the front (colored) side of the mat. With your sharp pencil in the outermost liner hole at the end of the extension, draw a circle (**Diagram B**).

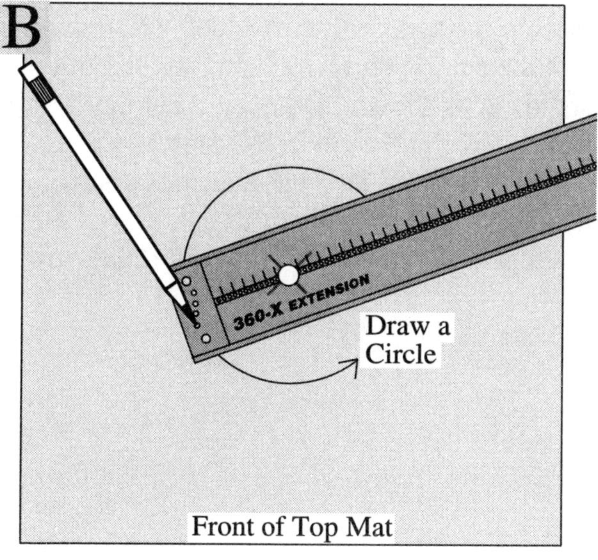

3 **Set the 4501 or 4505 dimensioning system at 5-1/8".** Draw a line at the top and bottom of the circle you just drew. Rotate the mat 90° and draw two more lines as shown (**Diagram C**).

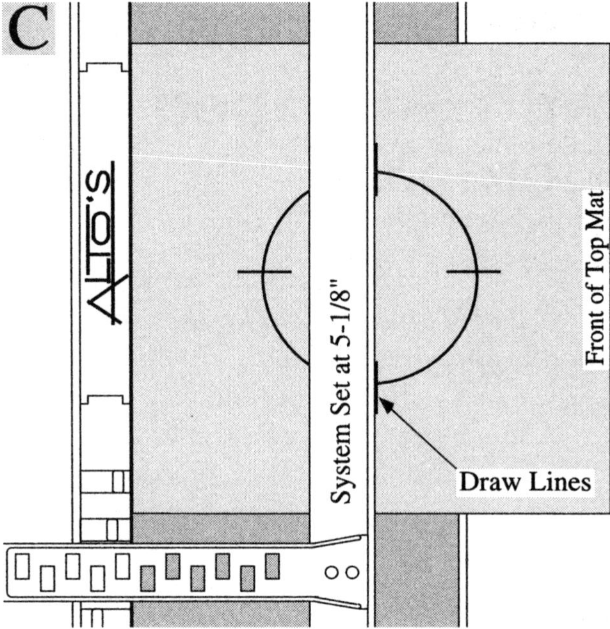

4 **Draw four more lines around the circle at 45° angles.** Place your ruler or straightedge corner to corner on the mat, and draw four lines as in Step 3 (**Diagram D**).

5 **Poke a hole through the mat at each place where the short lines cross the circle (Diagram D).**

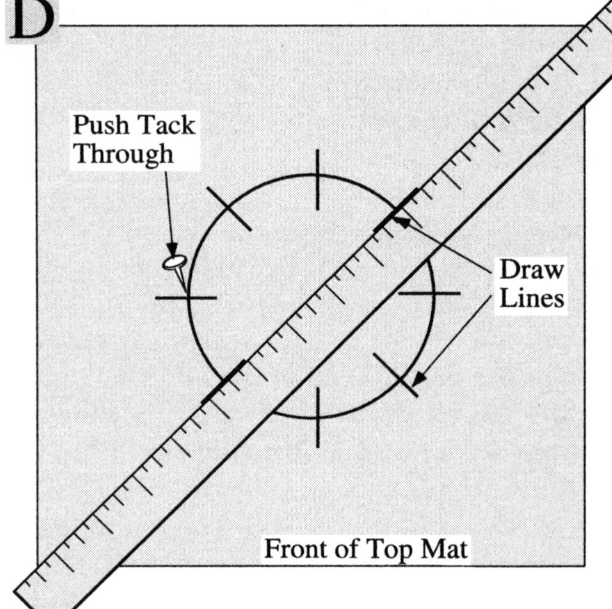

6 **Place the tack in the 2-1/4" hole of the Model 360.** Begin with any of the holes made in Step 5, by placing the tack with the Model 360 through the hole, into the cutting surface. In one fluid motion, make an arced cut as shown. <u>Do not cut out the complete circle.</u> Begin and end the cut in the center section of the mat. Continue around the mat in a clockwise direction, making a total of eight arced cuts. After eight cuts, the scalloped window should fall out (**Diagram E**).

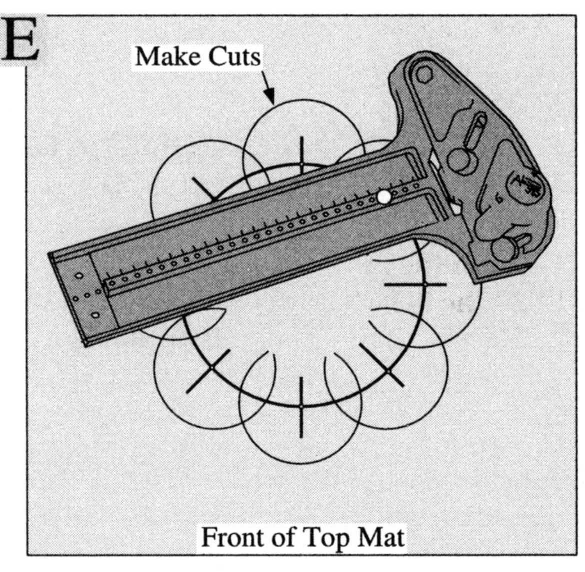

        Design: Scalloped Border

BOTTOM MAT

7 **Place the tack in the 4-1/2" hole of the Model 360.** You may use the 4-3/4 hole if you wish to have less bottom mat showing. Place the tack with Model 360 through the center hole in the other 10" x 10" matboard, into the cutting surface. Cut out the circular window **(Diagram F)**.

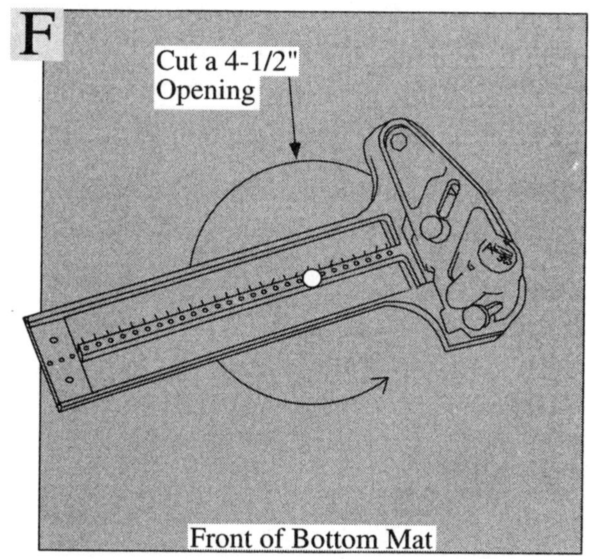

LAY OUT & CUT SCALLOPED INSERTS

8 **On the front of the third piece of matboard, cut several arcs around the perimeter of the matboard with the tack in the 2-1/4" hole of the Model 360 (Diagram G).** *Be sure to make the cuts so that the arcs' openings are facing the outside of the matboard, as shown.* Cut ten or more arcs so that you will have extras from which to choose the best pieces. The spacing of the arcs is not critical as long as they do not intersect.

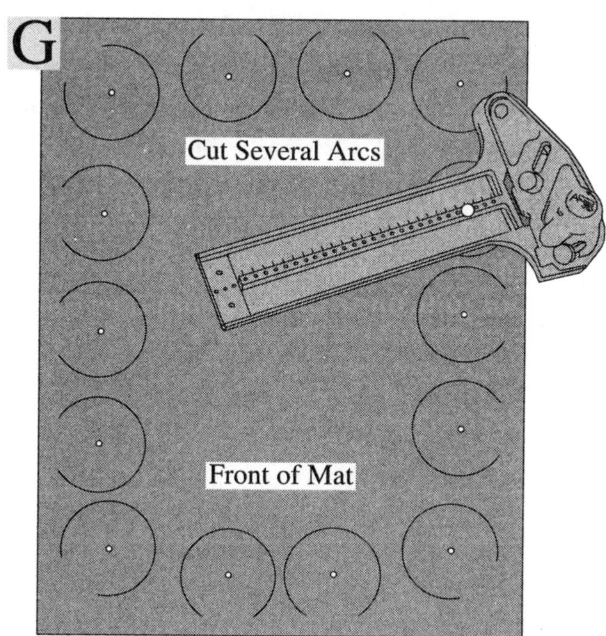

9 **Turn the mat over so that it is back side up.** With your ruler, measure and mark a spot 3-5/8" away from each pivot hole, as shown **(Diagram H)**. Draw a line from the pivot hole to this spot.

10 **Push the tack through the mat board at each of the 3-5/8" pencil marks you made in Step 9.**

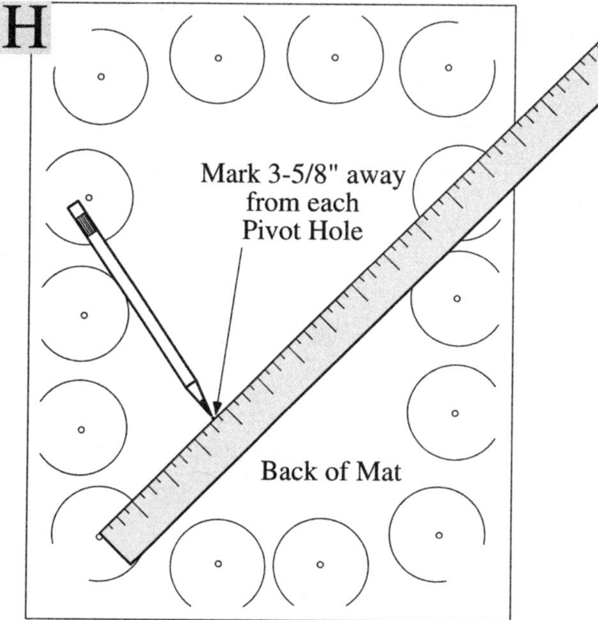

11
With the tack in the 6-1/4" hole of the Model 360, use the holes made in Step 10 as pivot holes to cut arcs, from the back side of the mat, through the cuts you made in Step 8 (Diagram I). Each insert should fall out. There will be extras, so use the best ones.

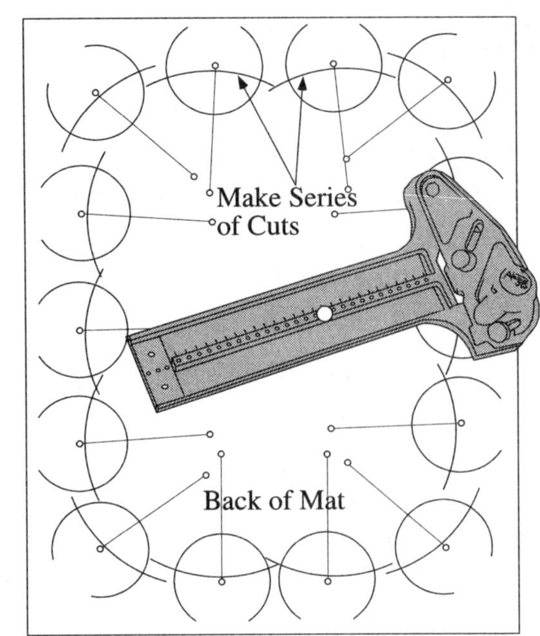

12
Assemble the mat. Align the top mat with the bottom mat, and adhere them together with double–stick tape. Use an acid–free white glue to stick the scallops into place as shown. Carefully align them in the spaces **(Diagram J)**. Be careful to not use too much glue, as it may squeeze out the side of the inserts onto the top of your mat. Once you have cut this mat, try varying the circle and arc sizes for different effects.

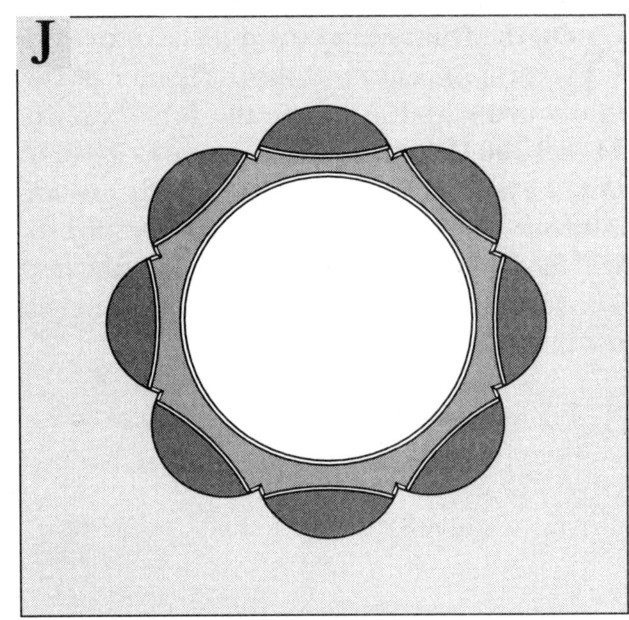

VARIATIONS

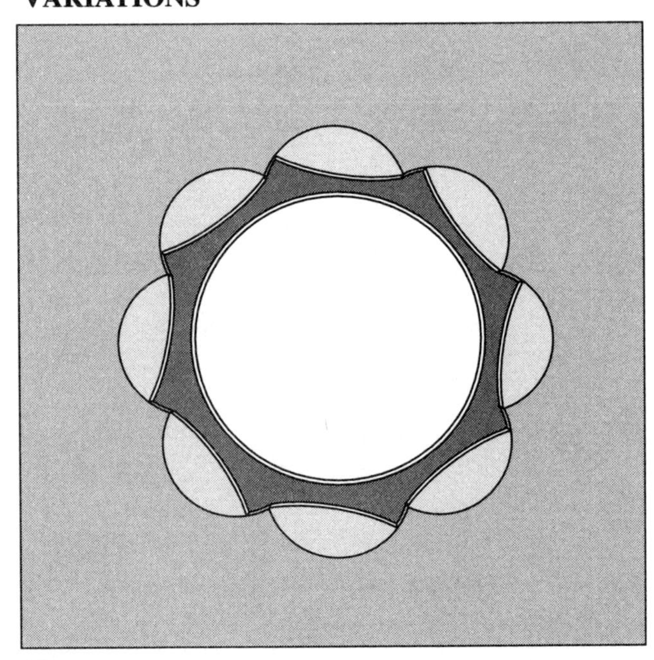

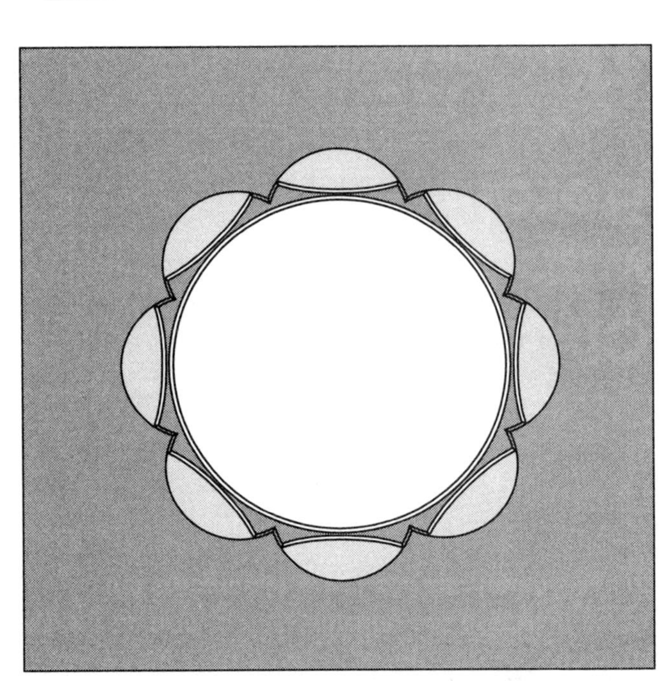

Design: Scalloped Border

Border Inlay

This mat, with the right inlay, can greatly enhance the elegant look of your art work.

Tools and materials needed
- Alto's 4501 or 4505 Mat Cutting System
- One piece of 11" x 14" matboard
- Sharp blade
- Sharp pencil
- Non–abrasive eraser
- Acid–free white glue
- 45°–45°–90° triangle
- One piece of decorative paper for the inlaid accents (at least 8-1/2" x 11")
- Sharp hobby knife
- Marker or pencil of similar color to the matboard.

1 **Begin by laying out the opening for the window of your mat.** With the dimensioning system set at 2-3/4", draw four start/stop reference lines on the <u>back</u> of your matboard **(Diagram A)**.

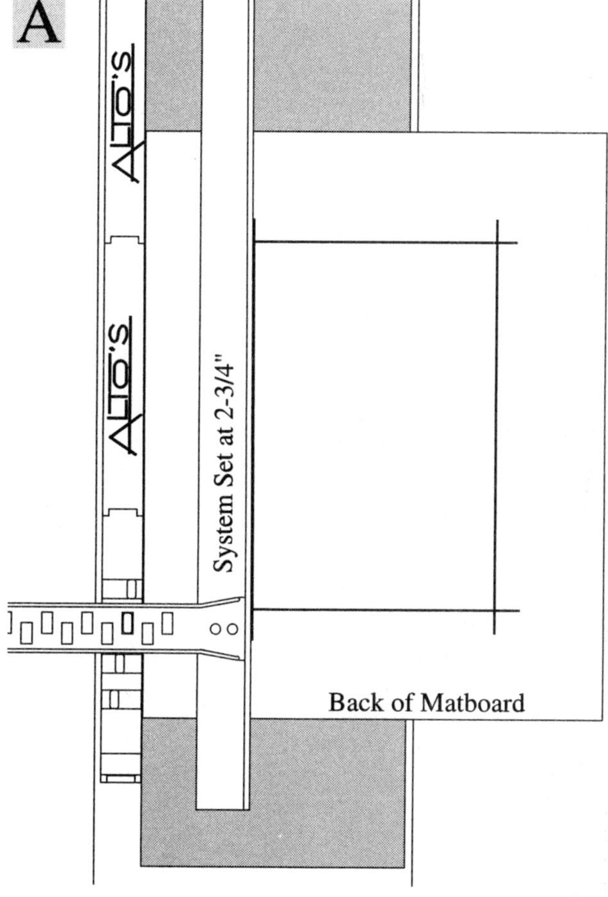

LAY OUT THE LOCATION OF THE INLAID STRIPS

2 **With the system set at 2", use your sharp pencil to lightly draw four lines on the <u>front</u> of the matboard as shown (Diagram B).**

3 **Set the system at 2-1/2".** Draw four more lines, again on the front of the mat **(Diagram B)**.
NOTE: After you become familiar with this mat you may find it unnecessary to draw the inner four lines. When you get to Step 5 simply set your system to the desired width and cut inside the pencil lines drawn in Step 2.

CUTTING THE CHANNEL FOR THE INLAID STRIPS

4 **Set the system at 2", and place the matboard face up, against the stops.** Using your hobby knife, carefully cut along the lines drawn in Step 2. Do not cut all of the way through the matboard. Only cut deep enough to go through the colored layer of the matboard. Cut all four outer lines around the mat. On these outer lines, avoid making overcuts at the corners **(Diagram C)**.

5 **Set the system at 2-1/2".** Cut along the remaining four lines as you did in Step 4. With these inner lines, however, make slight overcuts at the corners. This will ensure crisp inside corners in your channel. After making the cuts, carefully erase any pencil lines from the front of the mat **(Diagram D)**.

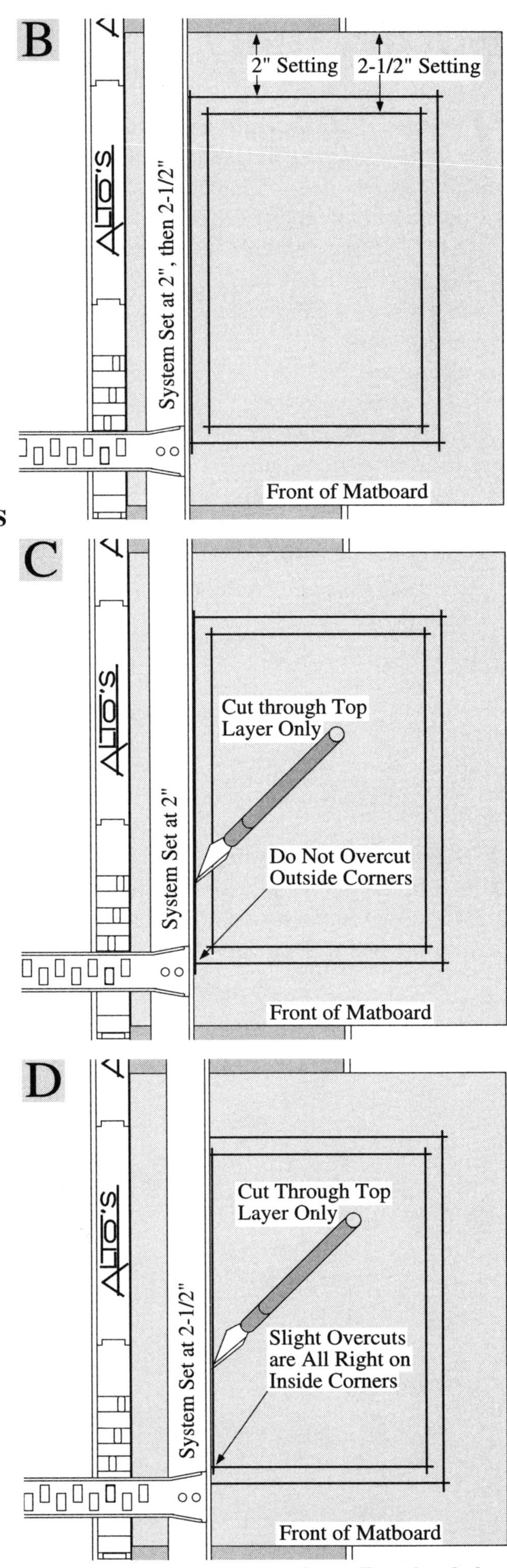

Design: Border Inlay

6 **Carefully peel the colored layer of matboard from between the two sets of lines you just cut.** Use the tip of your hobby knife to lift only the colored layer of the matboard enough so that you can grasp it with your fingers. Peel the layer off by lifting it straight away from the matboard as shown (**Diagram E**).

7 **With your marker or colored pencil, draw lines inside of the channel against the colored layer of the mat.** This will help mask any gaps that may remain after placing the strips (**No Diagram**).

CUTTING THE INLAID STRIPS

8 **Select a piece of decorative paper that is about the same thickness and weight as the colored layer of matboard you just removed.** Set the system at 5". Place the paper against the stops. Using your hobby knife, cut off a series of 1/2" strips by adjusting the system, i.e., make a cut with the system set at 5", then 4-1/2", 4", 3-1/2", and so on. Cut a few extra strips to have as spares (**Diagram F**).

PLACING THE STRIPS

9 **Carefully measure and cut a length of strip for the top side of the channel.** Leave the ends of this strip square. Apply a light amount of glue to the back of the strip. Mount the strip in place as shown. Repeat for the bottom section of the channel (**Diagram G**).

NOTE: Do not use too much glue. Excess glue may squeeze onto the front of your mat, staining it.

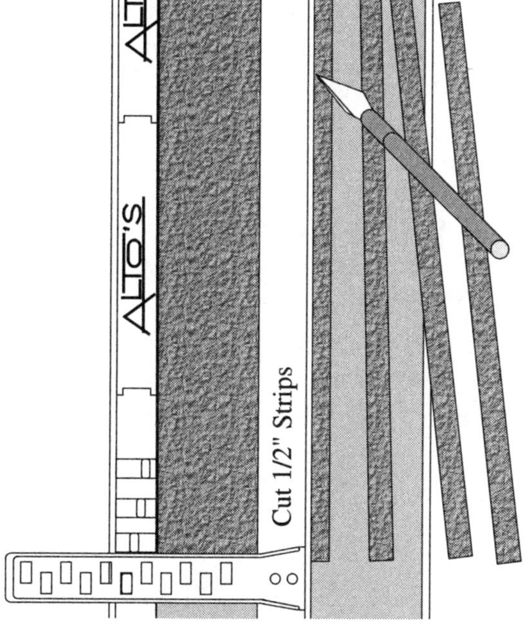

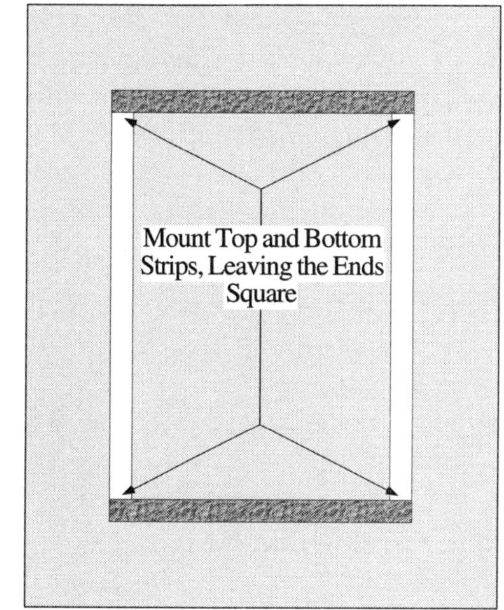

CUTTING THE SIDE STRIPS

10 **Lay a strip in the side channel so that it overlaps both the top and bottom strips.**
With your pencil, lightly mark the outer corner of the channel at each end of the strip (**Diagram H**).

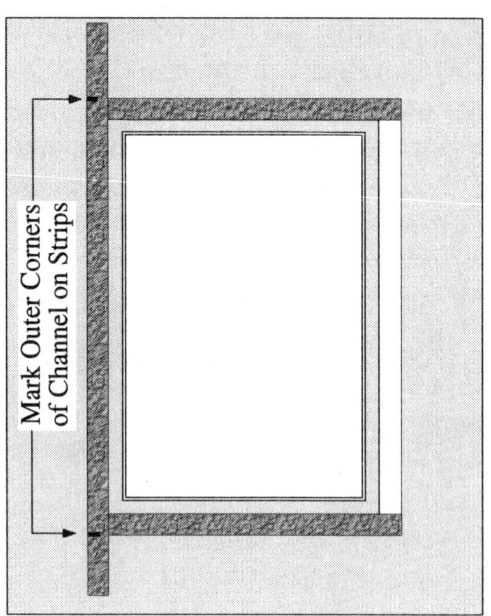

11 **Then, using your 45° triangle with the system, miter the ends of the strip.** Be sure to get the miter cuts in the right directions on the strip. Repeat for the other side (**Diagram I**).

12 **Glue the strips into the sides of the channel.** The mitered ends of these side strips should overlap the square ends of the top and bottom strips (**No Diagram**). **NOTE:** If the inlay material is not too thick you will get a cleaner corner by mitering only the side strips. With thicker materials you may want to miter all four strips.

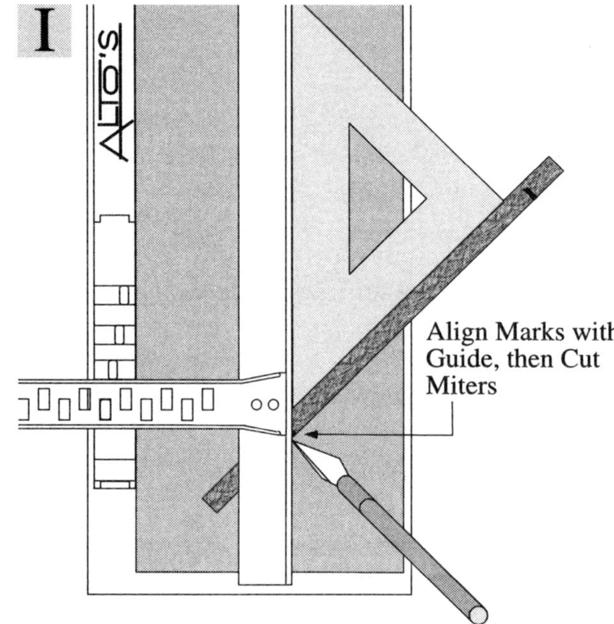

CUTTING OUT THE WINDOW

13 **Set the system at 2-3/4".** Place matboard face down under the cutting guide. Using your already drawn start/stop lines, cut the window out of the mat (**Diagram J**).

TRY THESE AND OTHER VARIATIONS :

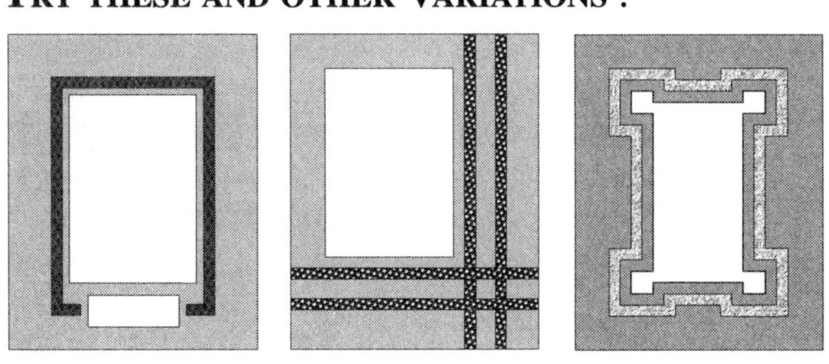

Design: Border Inlay

Freehand Cutting

*F*or this section, we will be discussing the *fundamentals of layout and cutting using freehand techniques.*

Tools and materials needed
- Alto's Model 30 Freehand Cutter
- Several pieces of scrap matboard
- Artwork around which to design your mat
- Matboard large enough for your artwork and the freehand design
- Sharp blades
- Sharp pencil
- Non–abrasive eraser

You may use freehand cutting by itself, or in conjunction with your 4501 or 4505 Mat Cutting System. The images we have chosen to use in this issue should be considered examples only. Freehand cutting can be applied to any mat you may want to cut. Imagination is the only limitation.

Before we begin, here are a few things to remember about freehand cutting:
- Push the cutter, don't pull it.
- Always move the cutter forward when cutting curves.
- Keep the bottom of the cutter clean.
- Always use a fresh, sharp blade.
- Use a non–abrasive eraser to erase any pencil lines.
- Don't feel like you have to follow the drawn lines exactly. Freehand cutting naturally lends itself to flowing, elegant curves as well as other design elements.

It may help to think of freehand cutting as drawing, done with a blade rather than a pencil.

CUTTING SIMPLE SHAPES

To gain some familiarity with freehand techniques, begin by cutting some simple leaf shapes.

1 **Cut the first curve.** This will be the right side of the leaf shape* **(Diagram A)**.

* For left–hand cutting, turn the blade around and Steps 1 – 3 will be cut on the left side of the design.

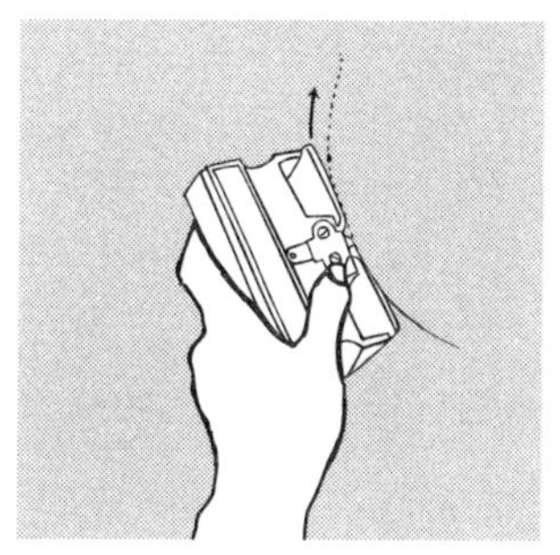

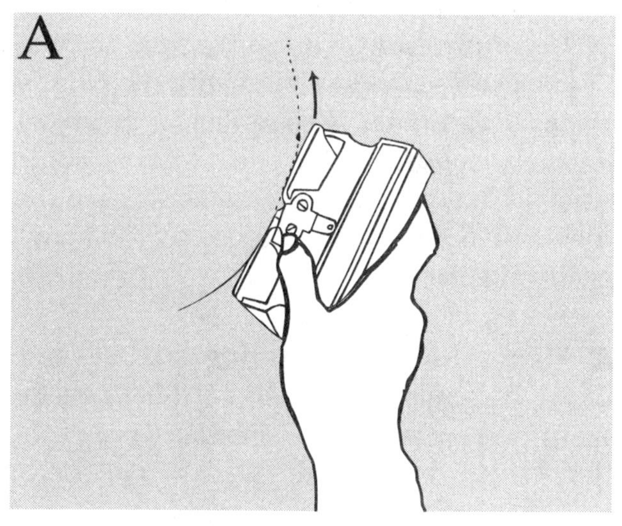

2 **Rotate the matboard 180°, so the first cut you made is now on the left.** For the second cut, start at the bottom corner of the leaf shape. Put the tip of the blade exactly where the first cut stopped. Slice the blade in at the corner and push forward for the other side of the leaf **(Diagram B)**.

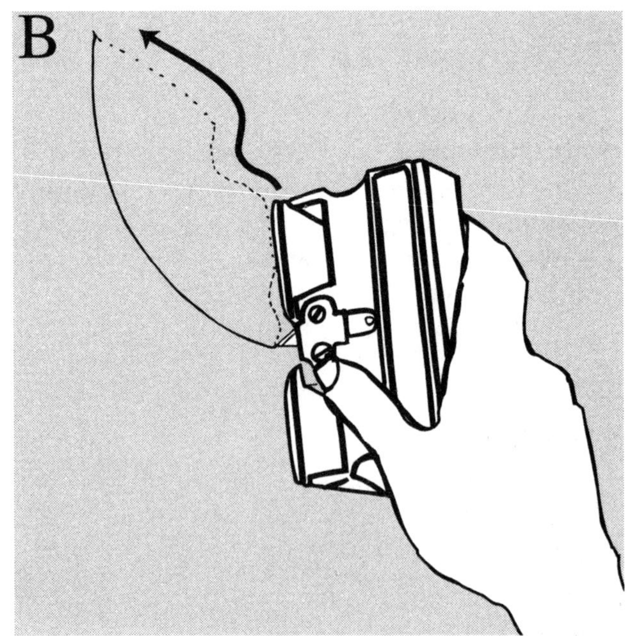

3 **Complete the second cut at the upper corner of the leaf exactly where the first cut started (Diagram C).**

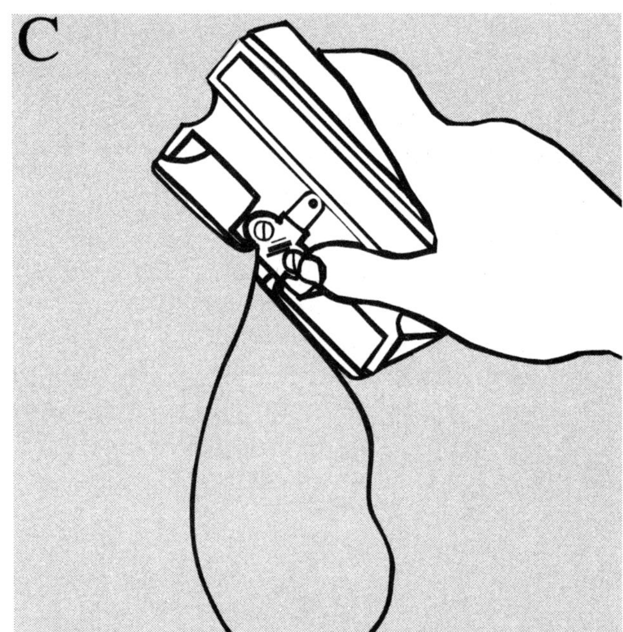

4 **Carefully remove the scrap from the center of the leaf by picking it out with the point of the blade (Diagram D).** Repeat Steps 1 through 4 until you feel comfortable using the Model 30 cutter in this fashion. As you practice, vary the size and shape of your cuts. Start with large broad arcs and proceed to smaller, tighter arcs.

5 **We at Alto's prefer cutting our freehand designs from the top of the matboard because the design being cut is clearly seen, since the base of the Model 30 doesn't cover your design as often.** See Step 10.

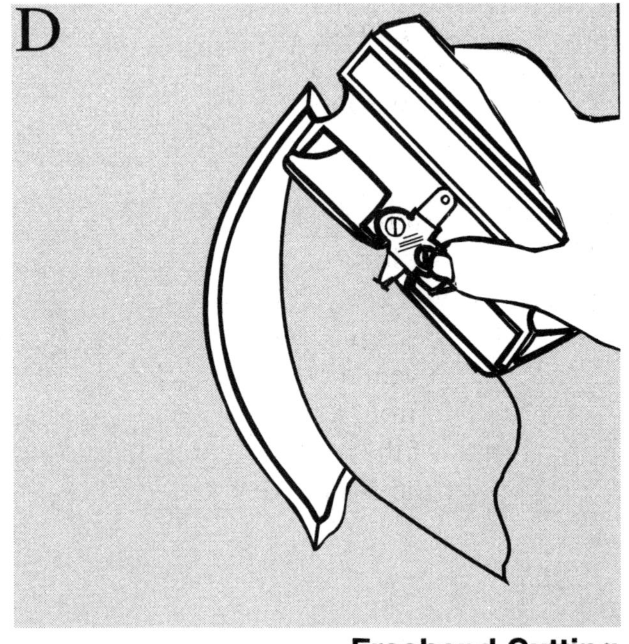

                                                  Freehand Cutting

6 **Before drawing any lines on the top of your matboard, take a scrap of the same kind of matboard, lightly draw pencil lines, then lightly erase those pencil lines.** You are checking to see if the eraser mars or damages the matboard in any way. If so, you'll have to draw your designs on the back of the matboard.

METHODS FOR LAYING OUT FREEHAND CUTS

STENCILS

7 **Preplan your mat border widths, leaving a space for the freehand design.** Cut the window first, and then locate the stencil on the top side of the mat in the border area. Draw lightly with a pencil around the stencil (**Diagram E**).

DRAWING AND CUTTING A DESIGN

8 **Lightly draw your design directly onto the surface of the matboard with a pencil** (**Diagram F**). Before cutting, it is a good idea to replace the window cutout so your freehand cutter will not fall into the opening. To cut, follow the guidelines given in Steps 1 – 5. Remember, cutting with a smooth flow is more important than staying exactly on the lines. After cutting, erase any remaining lines with a non–abrasive eraser.

CUTTING A DESIGN WITHOUT A GUIDE

9 **After cutting many designs, you will become familiar with repeated simple curves and shapes** that can be cut without drawing them first (**Diagram G**).

10 **Some kinds of matboard do get marked up when the base of the Model 30 runs over the top of it (dark brown matboard in particular).** If this is the case, a piece of paper over the mat may be sufficient to prevent these marks. If not, you'll have to cut your design from the back. When freehand cutting from the back of the matboard, you'll have to cut on the left side of the design, so your bevels are correct.

Some Freehand Cutting Ideas

Corner or Border Enhancement...

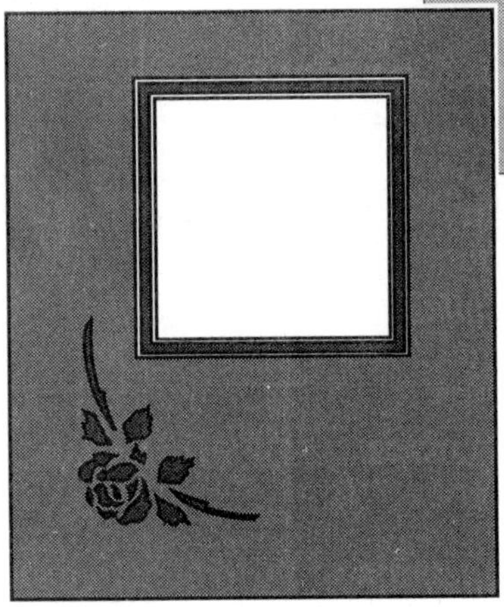

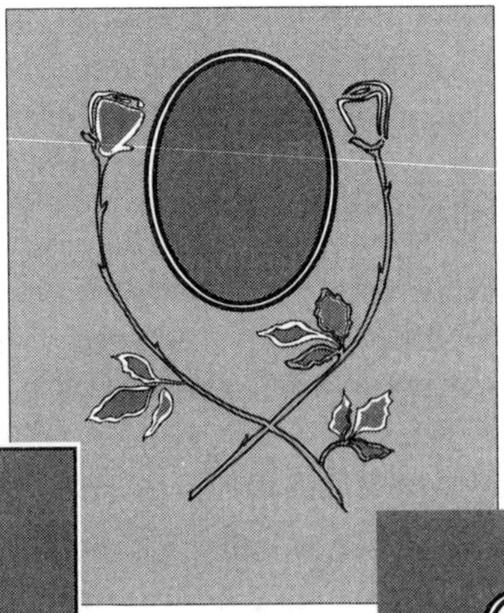

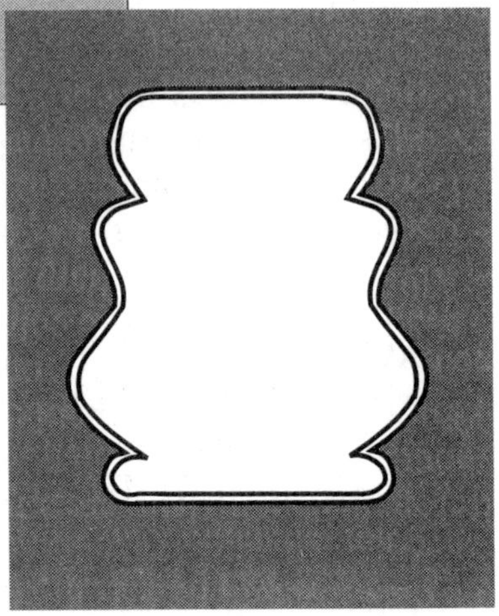

Artwork Design Elements, Double Mats...

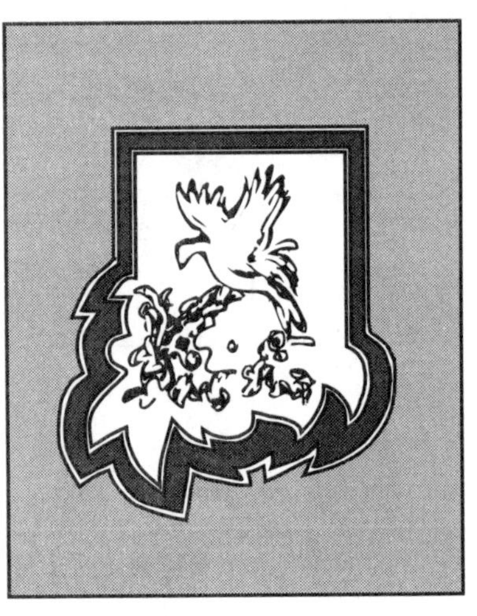

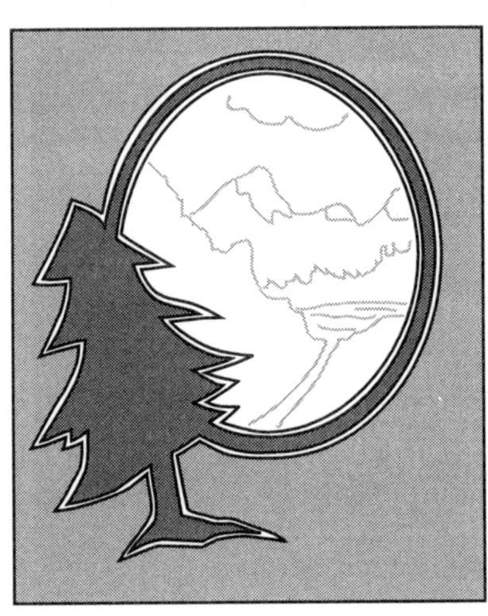

As we said earlier, freehand cutting lends itself to almost any matting situation. When thinking of a design for freehand cutting, remember that the design should support, or in some way enhance, the artwork you are matting. Is there a theme to the work that you may echo in your design? You may choose to repeat strong design elements within the artwork, or use the design to bring out other more subtle aspects of the work.

Often it is helpful to make a photo copy of the work you intend to mat, using the copy to sketch out several possibilities for designs before actually cutting. Above all, as with any fine tool, spend time becoming familiar with the cutter and how it works and feels. Eventually you will be able to realize your wildest design ideas.

Enjoy!

Inlaid Deco Corners

*T*his double mat is done in four stages.* First, lay out and cut the top mat, including several Far–Cuts. Second, lay out and cut the bottom mat. Third, lay out and cut the inlaid corners. Fourth, attach the inlaid corners.

Tools and materials needed
- Alto's 4501 or 4505 Mat Cutting System
- Two pieces of 11" x 14" matboard of different colors
- One piece of 8" x 8" matboard of a third color
- Sharp blade
- Sharp pencil
- Non–abrasive eraser
- Double–stick tape
- Acid–free white glue

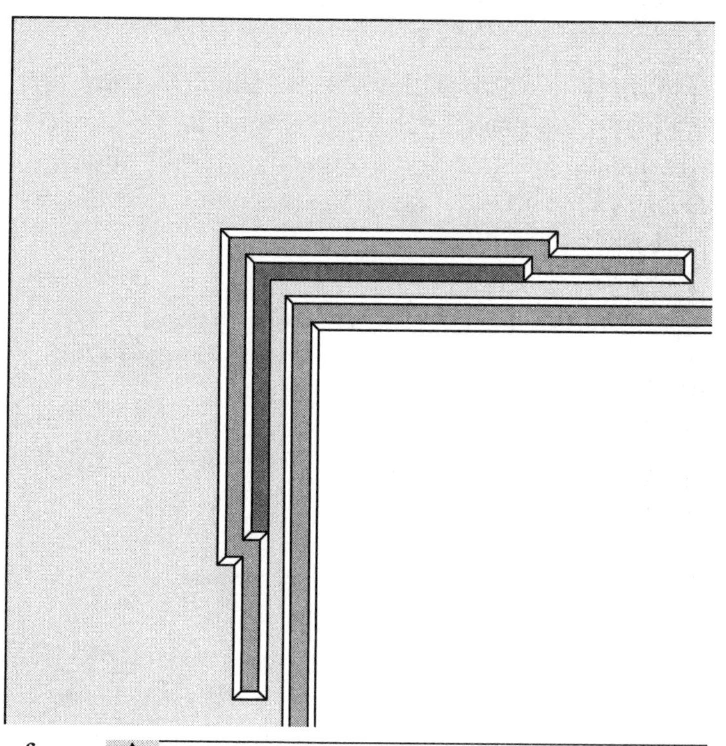

LAY OUT THE TOP MAT

1 **Set the dimensioning system at 2-1/8".** Draw four reference lines "A" around one of the 11" x 14" pieces of matboard (**Diagram A**).

2 **Set the system at 5".** Draw eight short lines "B" as shown (**Diagram A**).

3 **Set the system at 4".** Draw eight more short lines "C" as shown (**Diagram A**).

4 **Set the system at 1-3/4".** Draw eight lines "D" which connect the short lines "B" and "C" (**Diagram A**).

5 **Set the system at 1-5/8".** Draw eight lines "E". Be sure that the reference lines you have drawn on your mat match those in (**Diagram A**).

6 **Erase excess overlapping lines so each corner looks like Diagram A.**

7 **Label all of the Far–Cuts* with an "F."** There will be six Far–Cuts per corner, for a total of twentyfour (**Diagram B**).

*Far–Cuts are cuts made farther, or beyond, the standard reach[1] of the dimensioning system. For many of you this concept will not become clear until you actually do it. For this mat, there are <u>six</u> Far–Cuts in each corner and <u>four</u> on the inlay.

[1] The standard reach of the 4501 dimensioning system is 6". The 4505 dimension system will reach out to 8".

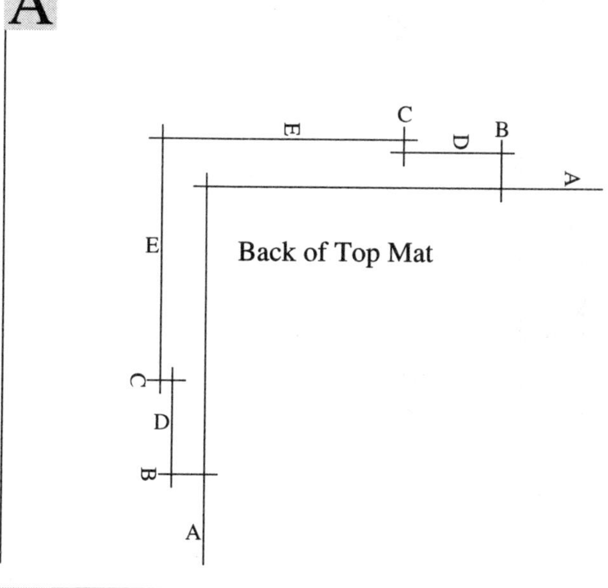

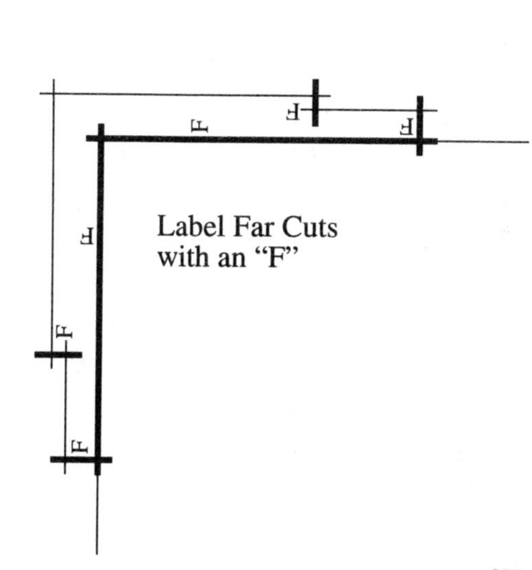

Design: Inlaid Deco Corners

47

CUT THE TOP MAT

The first cuts you will make are the Far–Cuts.
Far–Cuts are made by setting the system at 5", then sliding the mat over the stops and under the cutting guide. Line up the lines indicated in the chart below, and make the cuts as described.

8 **Make the following Far–Cuts.** Repeat the series of cuts for each side of the mat (**Diagram C**).

Line Up Lines	Cut From ---- To		Cut From ---- To	
B	D ------- A		A ------- D	
		halfway between		halfway between
C	E ----- D & A		A & D ----- E	
	halfway between			halfway between
A	E & A ----- B		B ----- A & E	

9 **Set the system at 1-3/4".** Make two cuts on each side of the mat. The first one, from about 1/2" before line "C" to line "B." The second, from line "B" to about 1/2" past line "C." Rotate mat and repeat cuts on each side (**Diagram D**).

10 **Set the system at 1-5/8".** Make two cuts on each side of the mat. The first from line "E" to line "C." The second from line "C" to line "E." Rotate mat and repeat cuts on each side of the mat (**Diagram E**).

11 **Set the system at 2-1/8".** Cut out the center window of the top mat, cut from "A" to "A" (**No Diagram**). *Before you cut out the center window of your top mat, you may want to review cutting double mats in your instructions* (see 4501 and 4505 Mat Cutting System Instructions, "Cutting a Double Mat – Method Two" p. 10).

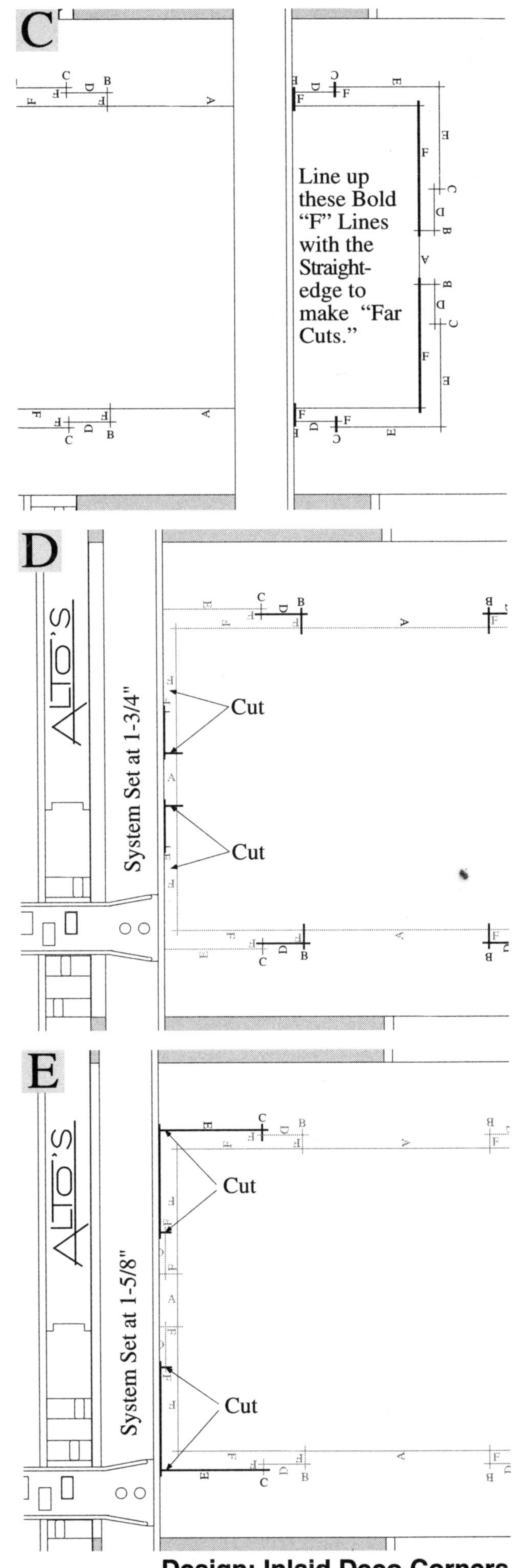

Design: Inlaid Deco Corners

LAY OUT AND CUT THE BOTTOM MAT

12 Cut about 1/2" off one end and one side of the other piece of 11" x 14" matboard and attach it to the back of the top mat, using double–stick tape (**No Diagram**). The bottom mat needs to be slightly smaller than the top mat.

13 Set the system at 2-1/4". Draw four reference lines around the mat. Cut out the window. Both the top and bottom mat window scraps should come out together (**Diagram F**).

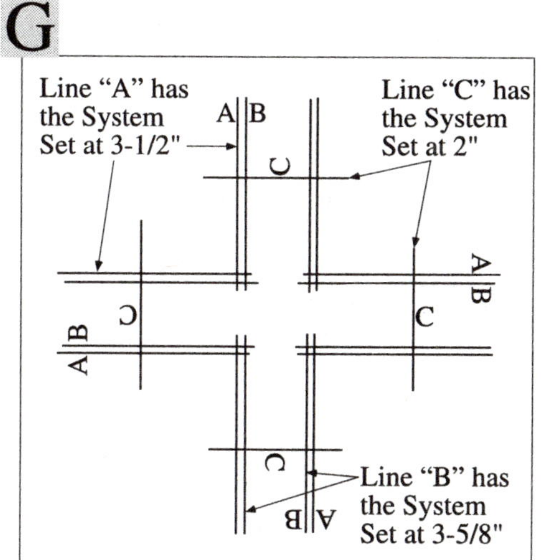

LAY OUT THE INLAID CORNER PIECES

14 Set the system at 3-1/2". On the back of your 8" x 8" piece of matboard, draw eight lines "A" as shown (**Diagram G**).

15 Set the system at 3-5/8". Draw eight lines "B" as shown (**Diagram G**).

16 Set the system at 2". Draw four lines "C" as shown (**Diagram G**).

CUT THE INLAID CORNER PIECES

17 Set the system at 5". Make the four Far–Cuts. Line up line "C" and make the cut across lines "A" and "B" (**Diagram H**). Repeat for each side of the mat.

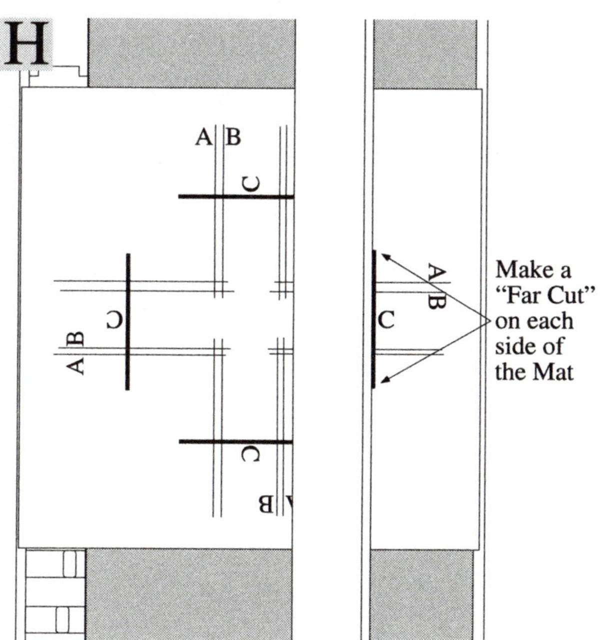

18

Set the system at 3-5/8". Make eight cuts, two cuts per side. First, from before line "C" to past line "B", then from before line "B" to past line "C" **(Diagram I)**.

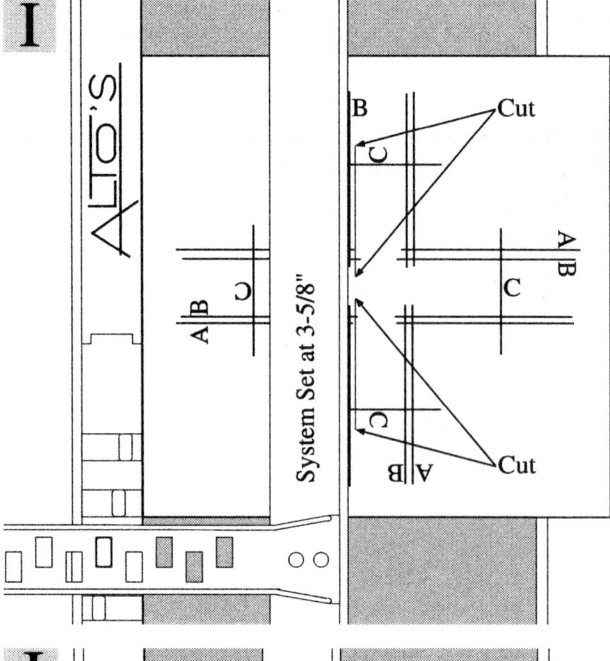

19

Set the system at 3-1/2". Make eight cuts, two cuts per side. First, from before line "C" to line "B", then from line "B" to past line "C" **(Diagram J)**. The corner pieces should now fall out of the mat. If there are any incomplete cuts, carefully finish them with a sharp blade (see Diagram G on page 4).

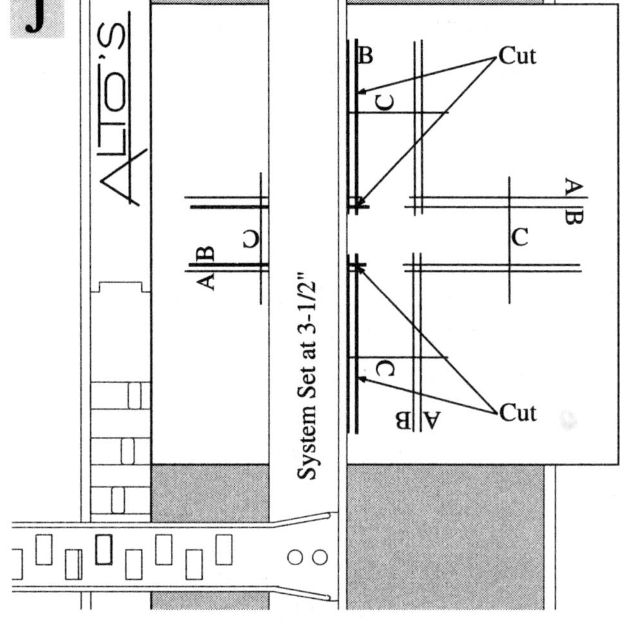

ATTACH THE INLAID CORNER PIECES

20

Carefully glue the corner pieces into the double mat corner openings, one per corner (Diagram K). Use only a tiny amount of acid–free white glue, being careful not to get the glue on other parts of the mat.

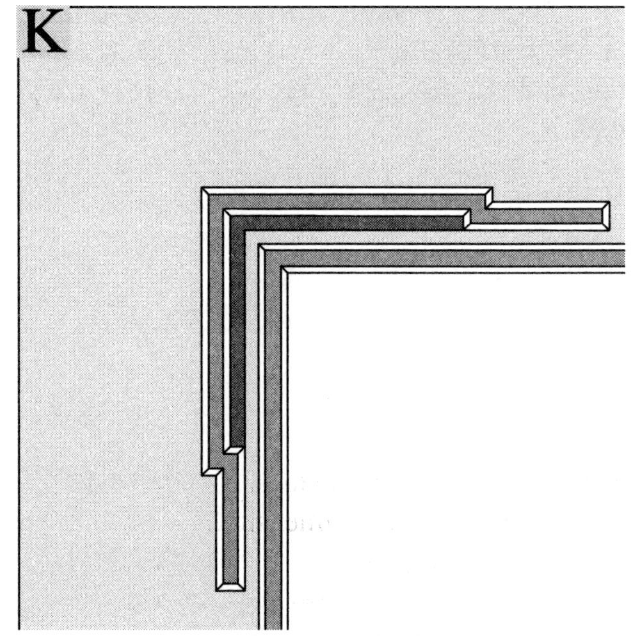

Design: Inlaid Deco Corners

Double–V Corners

This double mat is done in a couple stages. First, lay out and cut the top mat, including the Double–V's. Second, lay out and cut the bottom mat.

Tools and materials needed
– Alto's 4501 or 4505 Mat Cutting System
– Two pieces of 11" x 14" matboard of
  different colors
– Sharp blade
– Sharp pencil
– Non–abrasive eraser
– Double–stick tape
– Acid–free white glue

In this mat design, you will again be using the Far–Cut* technique. While it may seem difficult at first, with practice this technique will become natural.

1 **Set the dimensioning system at 2".** On the back of the top mat, draw two reference lines "A" as shown (**Diagram A**).

2 **Set the system at 2-1/2".** Draw two reference lines "B" as shown (**Diagram A**).

3 **Set the system at 3".** Draw two more reference lines "C" as shown (**Diagram A**).

4 **Set the system at 6".** Draw two short lines "D" which cross lines "A" as shown (**Diagram A**).

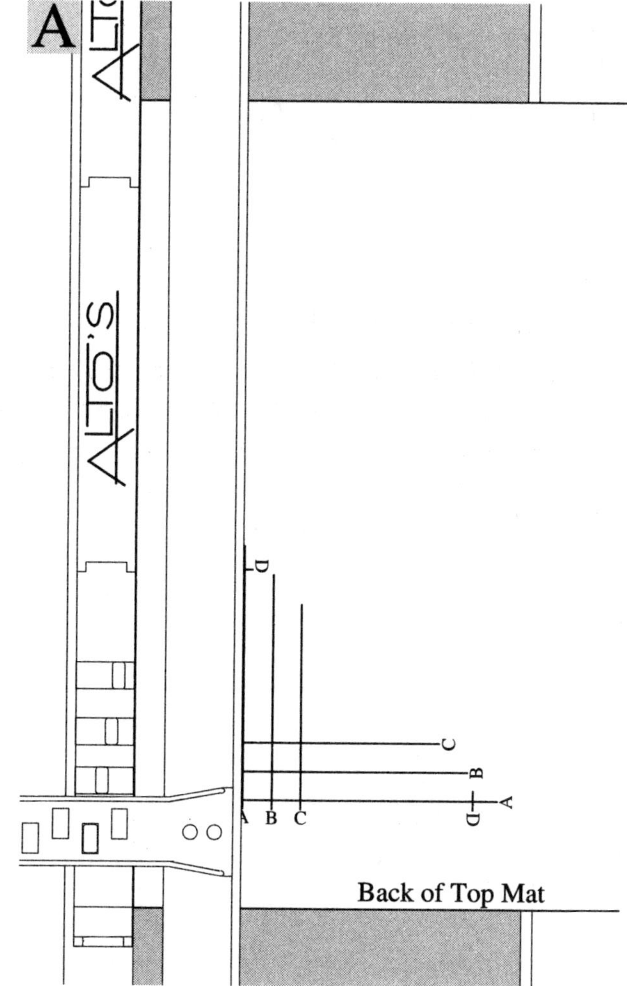

*Far–Cuts are cuts made farther, or beyond, the standard reach[1] of the dimensioning system. For this mat, there are <u>four</u> Far–Cuts in the "V."

[1] The standard reach of the 4501 dimensioning system is 6". The 4505 dimension system will reach out to 8".

Design: Double–V Corners

5 Erase extra lines in corner so that your lines resemble those in illustration (Diagram B).

6 **Set the system at 3-1/8".** Draw four reference lines as illustrated for the center window opening. To avoid confusion, do not draw the lines all the way across lines "A", "B" and "C." Draw shorter lines at the edges of the mat where the longer lines would have gone, as illustrated (**Diagram B**).

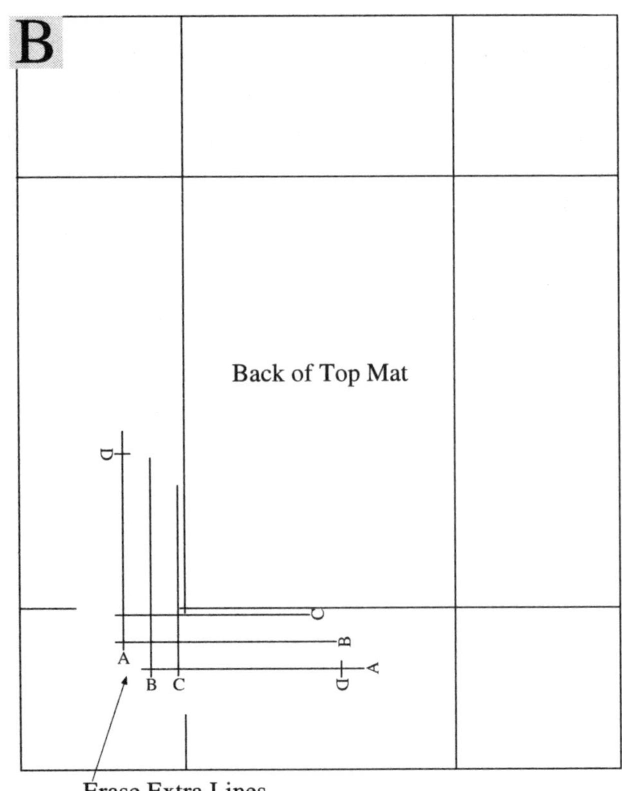

7 **Set the system at 5-1/2".** Place the matboard over the stops and under the cutting guide as shown. Line up the intersections of lines "D" and "A" with the cutting guide as shown. Draw two short lines which cross each set of three lines on each side of the corner. Label these lines "E." The bulk of the matboard should be over the stops (**Diagram C**).

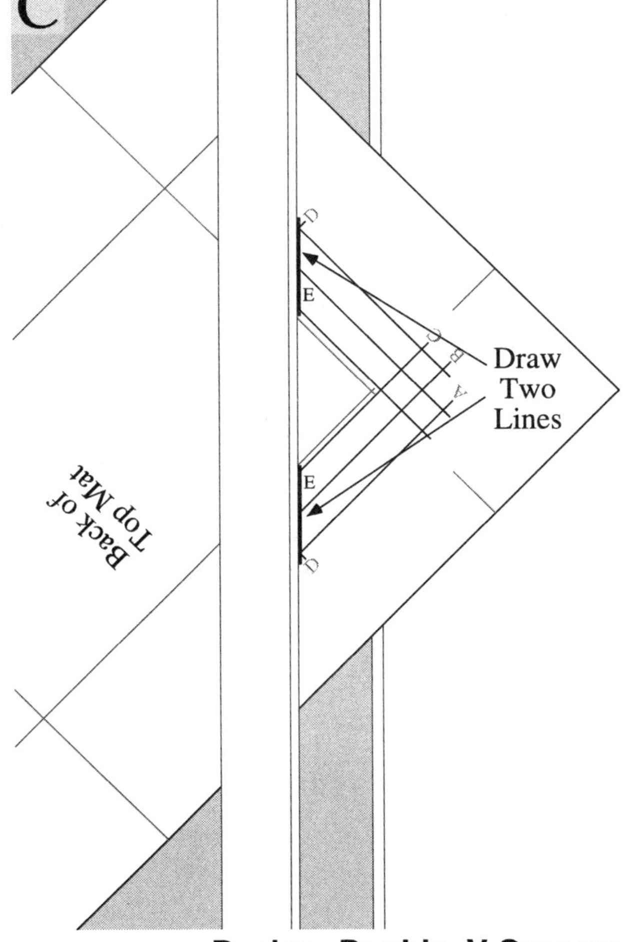

   Design: Double–V Corners

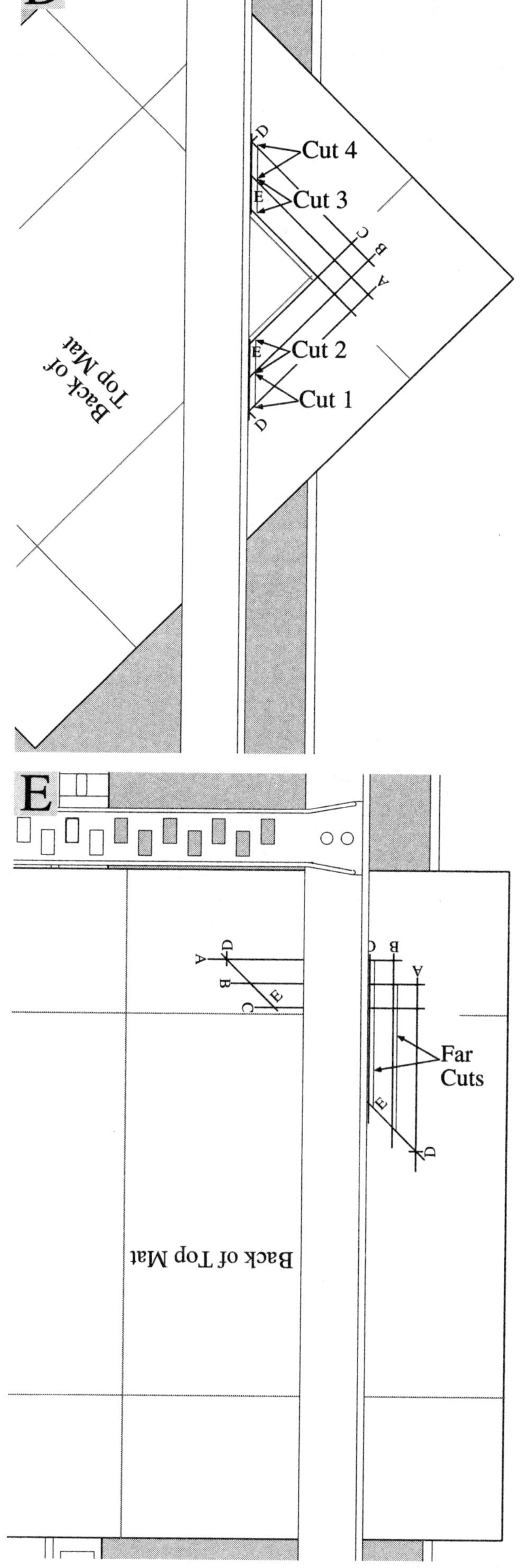

8 **With the matboard still in the system as in Step 7, make four short cuts as indicated in the chart below.** You will be cutting to and from line "B", so be careful not to overcut the line. Stop your cut with the blade edge just before line "B", then start the next cut with the blade tip on the same line **(Diagram D)**.

Cuts: 1. From line "A" to just before line "B."
          2. From line "B" to just before line "C."
          3. From just past line "C" to line "B."
          4. From just past line "B" to line "A."

MAKE THE FAR–CUTS

9 **Set the system at 5-1/2.** Place the matboard over the stops and under the cutting guide as shown, with line "C" lined up against the cutting guide. Make a cut from just past line "E" to just before line "A." Slide the matboard over so that line "B" is lined up against the cutting guide. Make a cut from just past line "E" to just before line "B" **(Diagram E)**.

10 **Rotate the mat 90°, and line up line "C" against the cutting guide.** Make the Far–Cut from just past line "A" to just before line "E." Slide the mat over to line up line "B" against the cutting guide. Make a Far–Cut from just past line "B" to just before line "E" **(No Diagram)**.

Design: Double–V Corners

11 **Set the system at 2".** Cut from line "B" to line "E" **(Diagram F)**.

12 **Set the system at 2-1/2".** Make the cut from line "A" to line "E."

13 **Rotate the matboard 90° clockwise and make similar cuts at the settings in Steps 11 and 12.** You will be cutting from line "E" to "A" at 2-1/2", and from "E" to "B" at 2". The corner pieces should now fall out. If there are any uncut corners, carefully finish them with a sharp blade, from the front of the matboard.

14 **Set the system at 3-1/8".** Cut out the center window. Leave the window piece in place for cutting the bottom mat. *You may want to review cutting double mats in your instructions* (see 4501 and 4505 Mat Cutting System Instructions, "Cutting a Double Mat – Method Two" p. 10).

CUT THE BOTTOM MAT

15 **Cut about 1/2" off one long side and one short side of the other piece of 11" x 14" matboard.** To secure the center "fingers" of the corner design, place a very tiny amount of acid–free white glue on the back of each one before attaching the bottom mat **(Diagram G)**. Attach the bottom mat to the back of the top mat, using double–stick tape applied to the back of the top mat **(No Diagram)**. The bottom mat needs to be slightly smaller than the top mat.

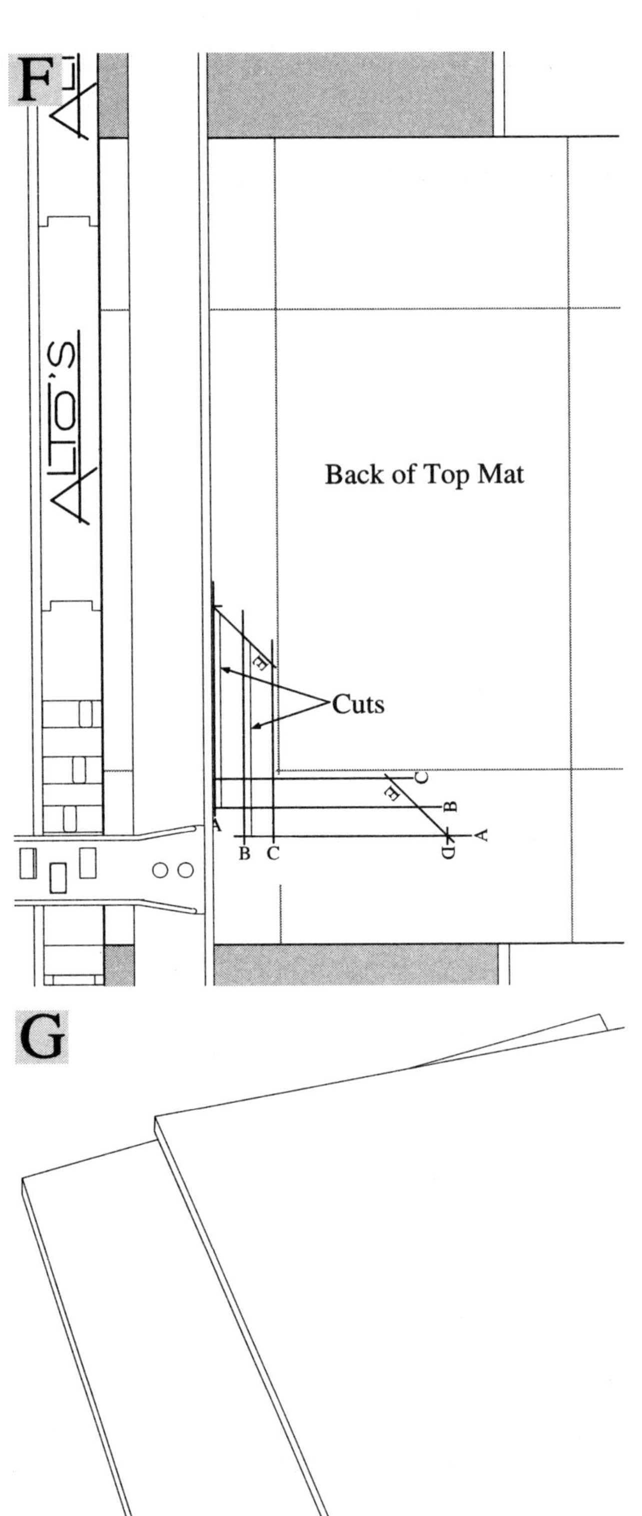

Design: Double–V Corners

16

Set the system at 3-3/8". Draw four lines around the bottom mat **(Diagram H)**. Leave the system at 3-3/8", and cut out the bottom window. Both the top and bottom window pieces should now fall out.

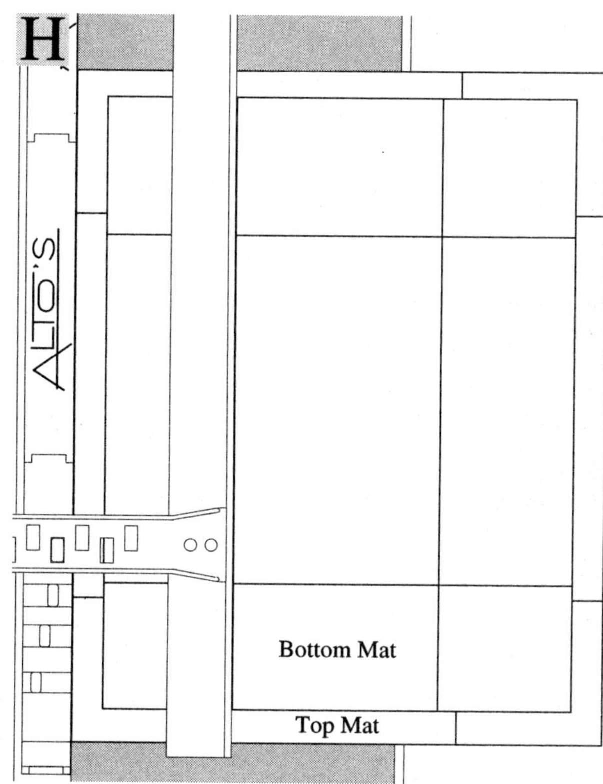

VARIATIONS

Once you have the basic concepts of this mat mastered, try some variations on the theme.

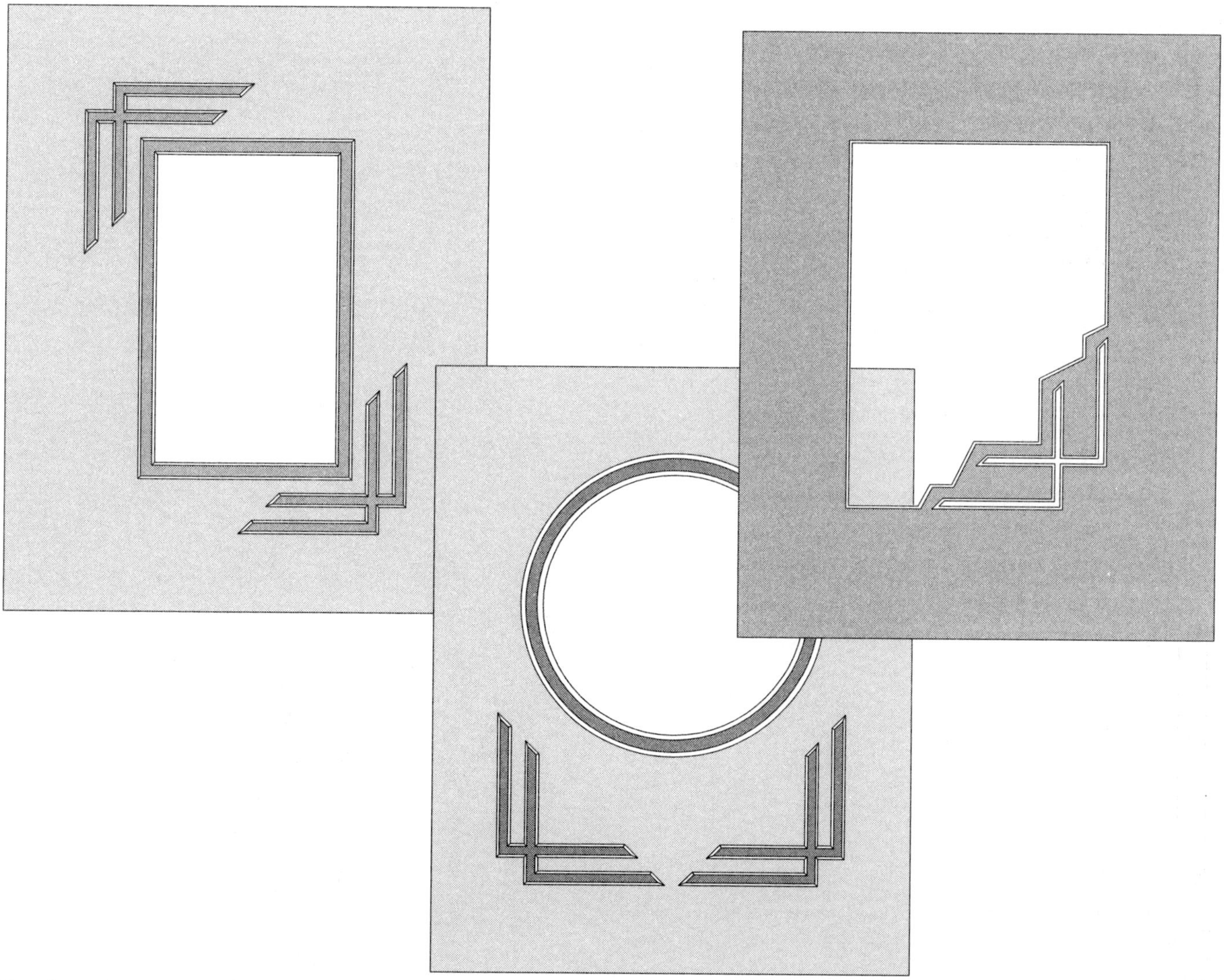